inspired
to
Quilt

inspired
to
Quilt

melanie testa

{ Creative Experiments
in Art Quilt Imagery

INTERWEAVE.
interweavestore.com

Editor, Rebecca Campbell
Photography, Larry Stein
Cover and interior design, Connie Poole
Production, Katherine Jackson

 Interweave Press LLC
201 East Fourth Street
Loveland, CO 80537-5655 USA
interweavestore.com

Printed in China through Asia Pacific Offset.

Library of Congress Cataloging-in-Publication Data

Testa, Melanie.
 Inspired to quilt : creative experiments in art quilt imagery /
Melanie Testa.
     p. cm.
Includes bibliographical references and index.
ISBN 978-1-59668-096-8 (pbk. : alk. paper)
l. Quilting. 2. Art quilts. I. Title.
TT835.T385 2009
746.46'041--dc22
                    2008052938

10 9 8 7 6 5 4 3 2 1

Acknowledgments

David, without you, none of this would have come into being. Thank you for your belief, trust, and love. You make my life a joy. You are my home. My person. My dream. Words do not suffice.

This book would not have come to fruition without the fierce love of my good friend Lisa Chipetine—thank you, Lisa.

It takes a mountain-top village to write a book. Alice Hill, Lynnae Ruske, Robin Sruoginis, and Sue Wilson, thank you for every helpful stitch. Thanks to Tim Williams, for helping keep my body aligned with my soul.

Pokey, thank you for asking me to join you for a glass of wine and for helping me get my act together. Rebecca, thank you for your kind prodding and gentle reminders. And to all the folks at Interweave, you all do fantastic work.

Last but not least, thanks to my Mom and Dad, for my work ethic and creative focus.

And thank you, good reader. Please remember it is not the supplies you collect but what you make of them. Make mistakes in blissful abandon; ease in the use of the media is your goal. Over time and with practice the wonder of the moment will shine through. Persist. Surround yourself in the works of artists greater than yourself, and you, too, will rise up among them. Start now.

contents

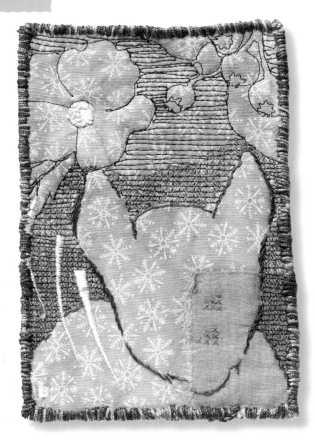

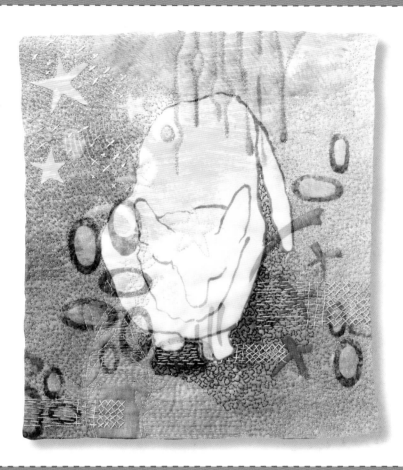

i love the accidentals. by this I mean
stuff like those odd heavy dots in the
largest flower. That was where the
paint peeled. I am learning
to get these effects on purpose!

My first quilting class was traditional, teaching me the Log Cabin, Rose of Sharon, and Grandmother's Flower Garden patterns. I learned strip piecing, appliqué, and piecing corners. I was asked to frequent our local quilt store, where I purchased my first pair of scissors, a thimble, and, need I say, fabric? The fabrics bowled me over. I can recall the layout of the entire store, and I was given lessons on how to audition fabrics by taking the bolts off the shelves and leaning my groupings together, squinting my eyes, and then removing and replacing them with new bolts. You know the story. I had been bitten—and hard!

Visual journals. These can be used as a place of release and relaxation and personal expression.

Sunday afternoons became my day to sneak away from the family meal and go over to the quilt shop as soon as I could. I was nineteen years old. I located a guild through the local paper and found myself at their welcome table, only to be told there was a waiting list to get in! I wasn't to be deterred; I planted my feet, not understanding why the event had been advertised, and was allowed entry. A niggling thought kept popping into my mind: how about going to school to become a textile designer?

Monthly I returned to the guild; each and every program was better than the next. I soaked up all the information I could. Then there was a business meeting. The main topic of discussion was whether to continue offering a scholarship, which was intended to help a future student enter into a textile-related field. A light went on. I researched what needed to be done to gather a portfolio together, bought the needed art supplies, and began drawing anything and everything. I had always been creative—but not necessarily focused. It took a few years, but I was accepted into the Fashion Institute of Technology's Textile/Surface Design program at the ripe young age of twenty-seven, with the scholarship of my first guild!

While there, I was taught to use liquid watercolor in fashion design and gouache for use in home decor. I was encouraged to keep a visual journal, where ideas, snippets of magazine pages, feathers, and drawings could be stored for future inspiration. I graduated two years later with an associate's degree.

If you have ever seen the movie *The Devil Wears Prada*, believe every moment of it. I was not fit for the competitive nature of the industry. So I found a job as a poster-restoration artist, where I furthered my skills in color mixing, utilized the availability of the works of art to saturate myself in the wide variety of drawing skills by the artists who originally drew and painted the posters. And I continued to journal. My drawing skills improved exponentially.

I took several classes by much-admired quilt artists in our community: Natasha Kempers-Cullen's Design and Composition, David Walker's Reverse Machine Appliqué, Ann Johnston's Stamping with Dyes, Carol Soderlund's Color Mixing for Dyers, and Jane Dunnewold's Complex Cloth. I loved taking classes, as I think many of us do, but there came a day when I was a bit confused.

Painting above, left side of binder, *The Old Couple* by Baptiste Ibar. Mixed media on canvas. 60" x 48" (152 × 122 cm).

I had a bunch of knowledge under my belt and admired the artwork of those who had so generously opened themselves and their approach to me. But I wanted to figure out how to take what I had learned and apply it to a style I could call my own.

So I dumped my fabric stash out into the middle of the living room; I folded, admired, and evaluated my burgeoning stash of hand-dyed, stamped, monoprinted, and bleach-discharged fabrics. Once all was organized, I took out my journals and slowly flipped through the pages. Cleaning and organizing has a magical effect; you clean the external world and new pathways open internally. Thoughts you might not have been able to access emerge.

I made a list that looked something like this:

Journaling Techniques	Quilting Techniques
Tracing paper	Organza
Painting	Direct-dye painting?
Collage	Collage: reverse machine, fusible web
	?
Hand drawn line	? Organza?
Transparency	Almost
Freedom	

Assessing this list, I saw that I had a few blanks to fill in but felt as though I had a clear mission. My goal was to create quilt art that accessed the freedom and playful spirit of the journaled page.

It was obvious to me that tracing paper and organza were in essence the same thing; up to that point, I felt more freedom painting on, gluing, and drawing over tracing paper within the pages of my journal. So I started to think about the differences and similarities between working on paper and working with cloth.

I assessed my resists. When working on paper, I used Frisket paper to block out and preserve areas of a design. Frisket paper is a clear, easily cut plastic paper that comes adhered to a paper backing that needs to be peeled away prior to applying it to the surface to be protected. It has a semi-sticky, removable tack that adheres to paper. Once it is applied, you can paint, airbrush, or stamp over the paper Frisket. The direct equivalent in cloth is freezer paper, which has a shiny surface on one side and can be adhered to cloth with an iron.

Then there is also liquid Frisket, which looks something like Elmer's glue, is a bit rubbery, and can be painted onto paper with a brush. Once it is dry, you can paint over it to your heart's delight. Afterward, the liquid Frisket can be removed with a rubber-cement eraser. The direct equivalent to liquid Frisket on paper is soy wax for cloth; when heated, this wax can be brushed or stamped onto the cloth, and dye or paint can be applied over and around the wax-resist area. Afterward, the wax can be removed by washing the fabric in hot water in your home washing machine.

It seemed I had almost all the pieces in place when I met a man who was organizing a figure-drawing studio and I was invited to join. I asked whether he thought it was okay if I were to bring my sewing machine, because I wanted to learn to draw directly using my machine. He said it wasn't an issue. This was hard to believe. I asked, "Are you aware that sewing machines make noise? And do you think the other people in the class would be bothered?" His answer was a simple, "Yes and no."

I had always known that I could draw with the sewing machine. I mean, that is what darning feet are for, aren't they? I suppose I needed to prove it to myself. I learned that contour lines (single, continuous line drawings) work best when drawing with a sewing machine. I used my fingers to indicate where I wanted the needle to end up; this helped me draw proportionately. The concept of drawing with the machine was exciting; the fact that I actualized the idea was very freeing.

Even though it took a few years of experimentation, this book is the result. I am now able to express the freedom and spontaneity of my journal pages—in cloth. I hope you, too, are inspired to embrace this approach, to begin journaling, mix and use color, and either paint on paper or dye on cloth. Learning to draw and mix color takes time. People tend to think either you have what it takes or you don't. This is a defensive statement, and it shields you from the work and play involved in letting go and just doing it. Allow yourself both the hard work and the happy accidents. Any and all experience gained will benefit your artistic endeavors.

So let's begin!

Arrow, my feline friend, is an inspiration and muse. He is used within the pages of this book to explore journaling exercises on page 51 and is featured on a Pretty Purse on page 111.

This chapter is the basis for all of the projects and ideas contained within the pages of this book. In this chapter, we will explore the means to make marks, apply color, and create cloth using Procion MX dyes on both cotton broadcloth and silk organza. You might use this chapter to make one-of-a-kind pieces of cloth for use in your art, or you can use these same techniques to create collaged whole-cloth wall hangings described in later chapters. Either way, familiarize yourself with the techniques in this chapter, and you will find new ways of combining the media and expressing yourself in cloth.

Moleskine Sketchbook journals, gouache, ink, and pencil. Daisies, above left. Art is like a muscle; use it or lose it.

Binders and Journals

Keep a binder of notes, snippets of your handmade cloth with simple notes as to how you made it, design ideas, sheets ripped from the pages of magazines, and doodles. This is an indispensable habit, allowing you access to process and approach for years to come. Without this hard-copy reminder, I assure you, over time you will forget what steps you took, and you will end up regretting not taking notes way back when.

In addition to keeping a binder with important design ideas, I also strongly suggest you keep an artist's journal. Over the past ten years, I have maintained the practice of keeping a journal, and much of my art draws upon and references those pages. Stamps sometimes mimic doodles. I'll project entire pages and re-create them in an art quilt, or I will pull disparate images from the pages of my journals and create a montage in cloth.

Visual journals keep you focused artistically even when you are unable to devote long periods of time in your studio.

You might purchase a journal that fits into your purse and carry one fantastic pen with you so that it's available whenever you think of it. Or you might purchase a journal appropriate for paints, a glue stick, and a mechanical pencil. Over time, and with practice, your journals will provide you with your own personal visual language.

I love working with gouache, an opaque watercolor. I carry a box of Pelikan opaque watercolor paints, a squeeze bottle to dispense water, a glue stick, a waterproof pen, and a pencil with me wherever I go. I am ready to draw or paint on a whim. My journal of choice is a Moleskine Large Sketch Notebook, which is specifically

formulated for use with gouache and acrylic. It has a pocket to keep small bits of inspiration in the back of the book and an elastic to keep it closed.

Studio Tools and Equipment

Be creative in acquiring studio tools and equipment. Reuse and recycle wherever possible. Being thrifty is an adventure. A good friend entered my studio a few months back and saw I was using plain rope strung over a couple of bookcases to hang my work to dry. This was distracting me visually, and I told her so. The next day she came over, power tools in hand, and strung a high-tension line intended to hang curtains over my sink. It stretches the length of the room and is high enough over the sink that I can continue to work without fear of getting my work wet.

Then there is my love of thrift and antique stores and, of course, eBay. The tools you can find to transfer soy wax to cloth are many and varied. You will be surprised by how many variations of potato mashers exist in this world! You will not be constrained by the wavy metal type we are used to buying in kitchen supply stores! Just do an Internet search for "primitive kitchen tools" and you will be off on a tangent that may make you forget to warm up the wax pot and get a creative groove on.

But on a more basic level, you can find a lot of what you need in your home or in a grocery or hardware store. For example, dishwashing soap comes in a squeeze bottle that is specifically formulated to contain a high-viscosity liquid, just like that of sodium alginate or thickener. Materials to make stamps can be found almost anywhere, from chair-leg protectors to drawer liners to string wrapped around Plexiglas. You just need to think outside of the original intention for the object at hand!

The following is a list of standard items you'll want to have access to in your studio.

16-OUNCE JARS: To dispense dye concentrate (jars with funnel lids are ideal).

RUBBER GLOVES: To keep dye from getting on your hands.

GALLON JUGS: To store liquid soda ash.

SQUEEGEE: To spread dye evenly across the back of a stencil or screen print. This evenly distributes dye over the surface of the resisted cloth and has a clean look.

JOURNAL: To store samples of dye processes, future design ideas, rip sheets, and the like.

MIXING CUPS: Anything can be used—yogurt cups, plastic cupcake forms, and anything you can mix in.

CLOTHESLINE AND PINS: To hang cloth to dry.

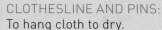

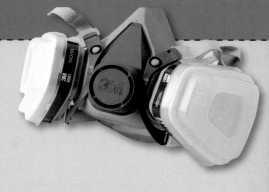

MSHA/NIOSH APPROVED RESPIRATOR MASK: A mask with filter cartridges is the safest mask and can be used to filter gases as well as airborne dust.

DUST MASK: For safety when using powdered dye and auxiliaries.

BUCKETS: To soak used foam brushes or stamps; these will help you clean as you go.

PRINT BOARD: A semisoft surface used for stamping, direct-dye painting, freezer-paper screen printing, soy wax, and many other printing techniques. Your surface should give a little when pressed and have the ability to be pinned into. It is also useful to be able to iron residual wax out of your print surface.

"T" PINS: Pinning your fabric in place on your print board will stabilize your cloth and enable you to print cleanly. This is especially helpful for techniques like stamping, screen printing, and direct-dye applications.

SMALL REFRIGERATOR: To store dye concentrate.

MEASURING SPOONS AND CUPS: To measure dye powder, thickener, and the like. Stainless steel or plastic are preferred. Do not use aluminum, brass, or copper as those may react with the dyes and auxiliaries.

RAGS: To clean your work area. Cloth rags can be washed and reused, an ecologically sound studio practice.

In addition to the tools and equipment, you will need several other materials in your studio to get started creating your fabric foundation.

Dye

Dye is a transparent medium; as a result, it has a luminosity and vibrancy that cannot be replicated easily in any other media. Because the dye particle bonds with the fiber of the cloth, it also has a great "hand," or feel, which is no different than how the fabric feels prior to dyeing.

Paint, on the other hand, lies on the surface of cloth, changing the hand of the fabric as well as the manner in which it handles when under the sewing machine needle. This is not to say that you cannot get beautiful results using paint. Due to its opacity, paint can provide a depth of layering that is essential to making exceptional cloth. Over the years, I have stayed away from using paint. Instead, to achieve an opaque effect, I use fabric collage between two layers of surface-designed cotton and silk organza.

Procion MX Type (Fiber–Reactive) Dye

MX Reactive Dye (Procion) is a dye specifically formulated to dye cellulose, or plant-based, fibers, such as cotton, rayon, and hemp, among others. Luckily, it can also dye protein fibers using the very same methods that are used for cotton. Heat is not necessary to bond reactive dyes to silk.

Dye Concentrate

With refrigeration, dye concentrate can be stored for three or four weeks, depending on the climate in which you live, and will retain full saturation of color during that time. Afterward, the dye will begin to break down, losing color saturation. Your cloth will look chalky and pale in comparison to newly mixed dyes. A small box refrigerator in your studio space is a necessity.

I know this is a seemingly obvious statement, but dye concentrates are highly concentrated and should be used as such. For example, when mixing a specific color, ask yourself whether you want a pale or a dark value. Pale colors require less dye concentrate; dark colors require more dye concentrate and/or colors that complement

Tie this in ... Color Palette

Choosing a color palette is subjective. The colors chosen here are a great starting point for any textile artist, and they are pure pigment, not a mixture of several colors, giving a broad spectrum from which to start.

PRO Chemical & Dye and Dharma Trading are the two most prominent sellers of dye, supportive chemicals, and equipment to the artist and dye enthusiast. Both companies have extensive websites with helpful information on techniques, approaches, and safety instructions. Each has helpful and supportive staff that will assist with any questions you might have about their products.

MX Reference Name/Number	PRO Chemical & Dye	Dharma Trading
Yellow MX G	Sun 108	Lemon 1
Red MX 8B	Fuchsia 308	Fuchsia 13
Blue MX G	Turquoise 410	Turquoise 25
Yellow MX 3RA	Golden 104	Deep 4
Red MX 5B	Mixing 305	Light 12
Blue MX G	Intense 406	Cerulean 23
Yellow MX GR	Tangerine 112	Golden 3
Red MX GBA	Strongest 312N	Chinese 10A
Blue MX 4GD	Navy 414	Navy 24 (MX 4RD)

in order to darken the color. Urea water (see page 18) acts as white in color mixing with dyes. When you see a color you like, evaluate it. Ask yourself what the base color is, whether it is a light or a dark color, and whether you see any neutral tones. Take your color samples out and compare them to the color you are evaluating. Which color is predominant? Which other colors do you see within your sample?

It is my preference to mix color from the dye concentrates, squeezing some dye into a mixing cup, perhaps adding urea to lighten it, then mixing thickener into this, which will lighten the color a bit more. Remember that you can mix up to equal parts dye to thickener.

Newcomers to color mixing often shy away from the task. Don't! Instead, embrace color mixing as a means of creative expression. You will make mistakes; it is part of the process. But you will also gain knowledge by doing so. Work slowly and methodically, remembering that a little dye goes a long way.

Tie this in ...

Prolonging the Life of Your Dye Concentrate

If you are unable to obtain a refrigerator for your studio, find a plastic box with a tight-fitting lid, just large enough to be stored on the bottom shelf of your family refrigerator and able to contain all of your dye concentrate bottles. This way, the dye is separate from your food supply and will not be confused as something that might be edible. Keep this box very clean, both inside and out, and label it in no uncertain terms.

MIXING DYE CONCENTRATE
To mix dye concentrate, you'll need a funnel, a jar, water, and urea pellets. Using a funnel, put 2 tablespoons of urea pellets in a 16-ounce jar. Add cup of hot water, cover, and shake until dissolved. Add 1½ tablespoons of dye powder and 1½ cups of water to the jar, cover, and shake again.

Tip **Getting Good Results**
To get predictable results when mixing dye concentrate, I suggest you weigh your dye rather than measure it by the tablespoon. The reason for this is that each dye has a different volume per weight; some are fluffy, while others are dense. For example, 1 tablespoon of fuchsia will not weigh the same as 1 tablespoon of navy. Use a 5 percent solution, 5 grams of dye per 100 ml water.

Experiment!

Mix equal parts of thickener to dye concentrate, 1 teaspoon of dye to 1 teaspoon of thickener. :: Take a soda-soaked (see page 19) piece of cloth and squeegee each color off the edge of the cloth. Place the colors in groupings, with reds, blues, and yellows together. In this way, you will have a permanent reference of each color. Batch (see page 19), wash, and store in your three-ring binder.

Print Paste

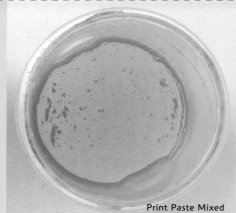

Print Paste Mixed

Urea

Urea is a synthetic humectant (a substance that helps absorb and retain moisture). Urea helps cloth stay wet, allowing the dye a longer period to bond with the fibers of the cloth. Urea water also acts as white when color mixing and can be used to lighten the value of the dye prior to mixing it with thickener. Add 3 tablespoons of urea to 8 ounces of hot water and shake well. Open with care, because a chemical reaction can pressurize the closed bottle after shaking.

Thickener or Print Paste

The terms thickener and print paste are used interchangeably. There are several types of thickeners on the market sold under several names and indicators. The basic difference allows for either a high viscosity (SH, HV), used for cotton, or a low viscosity (F, LV), used for silk, nylon, and synthetic fabrics. Lowering the viscosity of the thickener allows you to obtain more precise lines. In other words, silk, nylon, and synthetic fibers accept liquid more readily than does cotton, and, as a result, require a thinner application of thickened dye.

The primary ingredient to thicken dye is called sodium alginate, which is derived from seaweed. It is a food-grade thickener and can be used by itself or as part of a mixture that also contains urea and Metaphos (a water softener). Urea encourages the fabric to stay wet longer, while the water softener acts as a conditioner, helping you obtain a smoother paste more quickly.

A little bit of sodium alginate goes a long way. If you choose to purchase straight alginate, mixing it with an electric blender will speed the process considerably. I chose to use Pro Print Paste SH (a mixture of sodium alginate, urea, and water softener) early in my artistic development and made

the assumption that I could use it for both silk and cotton fabrics. I like the consistent results I get when mixing the recipe (page 17). I mix it thinner than the manufacturer suggests. This is simply my preference. You should purchase any of the configurations sold that you find work for you.

In order to mix thickener, slowly add 11 level tablespoons of Pro Print Paste SH to 2 cups of hot water while stirring. Continue stirring until a smooth paste is obtained. Let stand for at least 1 hour for smoothest results.

When mixing thickener to dye, you will want to obtain a consistency of heavy cream. Your mixture should easily flow off your mixing utensil. A good starting point is that you can mix up to equal parts of dye to thickener.

Dye concentrate in a funnel-type bottle.

{ ***Tip*** **Storing Print Paste**
Store dry print paste mix in an airtight container. Liquid print paste can last for months when refrigerated; without refrigeration, however, the paste will eventually become moldy. To thin print paste, add urea water (see page 18) until the desired consistency is obtained.

Soda Ash

Soda Ash

Soda ash is used as an alkali fixative for Procion MX Reactive Dyes. To use soda ash, you'll need a gallon jug, ½ cup of soda ash, 3 tablespoons of urea (see page 18), and 1 gallon of warm water. Place the urea in the gallon jug first. Pour a small amount of hot water over the urea, cover, and shake. A chemical reaction will occur, making the hot water turn immediately cold, but this will also help dissolve the urea faster than if you had not used hot water. Carefully remove the lid, add the soda ash, fill the gallon jug with room-temperature water, cover, and shake until the soda ash dissolves. Soda ash can have the tendency to clump, so shake periodically while the soda ash is still dissolving.

Soda Soak

Soaking fabric, both silk and cotton, in a soda-ash solution is also known as soda-soaked cloth. Once the cloth is drip-dried, you can directly apply thickened dye to it. The needed reaction between the soda ash and the dye particle will occur as the thickened dye is absorbed into the fibers of the cloth and allowed to slowly dry, or "batch" (see below, right).

Do not confuse the terms prepared for dye (PFD) and soda-soaked cloth. PFD means that the cloth is free of whitening agents, permanent-press finishes, and fixatives, allowing the cloth to accept dye without hindrance. Soda-soaked cloth has been soaked in soda ash and allowed to drip-dry in preparation for thickened dye applications. We use PFD cloth, soak it in soda ash, then drip dry for all applications in this book.

Soak cloth for 30 minutes before drip-drying. After soda soaking cloth, you can funnel leftover soda-ash water back into your storage container and reuse it.

Be aware that not all fabrics accept dye. Some fabrics have finishes that prevent the fibers from accepting color. These fabrics will dye to a chalky, disappointing color. Purchase fabric from a source that caters to home dyers and textile artists (see Resources, page 134). Bleached, mercerized combed cotton broadcloth has a sturdy and dense weave. It accepts and reflects dye vibrantly. Silk organza 5.5 mm (mm, or

mommes, is a silk measurement of weight, similar to thread count in cotton; organza runs from 4 to 6 mm) is sheer, has a crisp hand, and is sturdy. It accepts and reflects dye vibrantly. Organza tends to shrink by about 6 percent both warp and weft, so cut your organza slightly larger than your finished dimensions.

Ironing soda-soaked cloth is necessary because creases and wrinkles will be accentuated during the printing process. Iron soda-soaked cloth gently but quickly; use the setting just below cotton. Soda ash is flammable, so quick, firm strokes with your iron will do the trick. No need to use a Teflon sheet; just be aware of the limitations of the media. Never dry your soda-soaked fabric in a clothes dryer; it is flammable and will ignite under such conditions.

BATCHING

Place your completed soda-soaked work between layers of plastic and allow it to sit for at least 24 to 48 hours. This helps slow the drying process and allows the dye particles time to bond with the fibers of the cloth. The optimal batch temperatures for both cotton and silk are 95° to 105°F (35° to 40°C). After this period, you can wash with Synthrapol or textile detergent (see Safety and Studio Practices, page 128), dry, and use your cloth.

Synthrapol or Textile Detergent

Synthrapol or textile detergent are types of soap that isolates and removes dye particles. They are the recommended soap for the final wash of your dyed cloth. Both cotton and silk can be washed in the same manner. It is a good idea to separate your darks and lights and wash them separately. Soak your dyed items several times in cold water until the water runs clear and then wash in hot water using Synthrapol or textile detergent.

Now that we have covered the basic tools, equipment, and materials, we are ready to move on to how to use thickened dyes to make cloth. Each application will be discussed in detail. Explore the applications and experiment with ways to combine them. Making cloth with depth and dimension is the goal.

Cotton broad-cloth stamped with cardboard stamp, applied freezer paper Xs, monoprint, and stamped purple Xs.

Printmaking

Three main factors contribute to successful designs: color, dimension, and texture. Color is the main draw in successful designs. It will draw the viewer in and create a dialogue. Differences in scale of motif (dimension) are also important. Large motifs jump to the foreground; small motifs recede. Add texture (and differences in texture) to this equation, and you will create successful cloth.

Stamping

Stamping can be an adventure when printmaking. Stamps can be used to add color, dimension, and texture. Drawer liners, glue, cardboard, string, packing foam, craft foam, Plexiglas, and bubble wrap are all fair game for making stamps. Some stamps can be made to last a lifetime, and others will remain in the studio until they become unusable, as is the case with cardboard and glue-type stamps.

Making and using your own stamps allows you to create a set of personalized designs that are unique to you. Some of these motifs will become synonymous with your quilt art; your art will become recognized by the motifs you use. And what is better than to be recognized for designs that were created entirely by yourself?

Before you begin making stamps, it might be a good idea to get out some paper and pens and allow yourself to gently unwind visually. Don't think of this time as anything more than a warm-up. Let your eyes, mind, and hand relax, and just doodle. Use thick markers; change over to pencil, and experiment to see what speaks to you. Many of my stamps originated from such doodles. If you find that you doodle when talking on the phone or while at meetings at work, it is time to start saving these little snips of paper and taping them into the pages of your journal. Better yet, carry your journal with you wherever you go and doodle directly in it.

Stamps are a fun and easy approach to making marks and repetitive designs on cloth. Each type of stamp I describe below adds a different look and feel to the finished print. Adhesive-backed craft foam and carved stamps have a solid, finished look, while glue stamps and cardboard stamps have an edgy, gritty type of print.

Before using stamped imagery in a piece, I ask myself what effect and emotional feel I am trying to convey. If I am looking for a clean, austere feel to the finished artwork, I will reach for craft foam or a carved stamp. On the other hand, if I am looking for noise and drama, my preference is the glue- or cardboard-type stamp.

Often, when I make stamps, it is because I need to regroup after making a large work of art; making stamps is a way to reconnect with my creative center. Because of this, I often make stamps without a specific purpose or goal for their end use. Using stamps is another matter entirely. When I reach for a particular stamp, it is with the goal of the artwork in mind.

Create several of each type of stamp and play with the manner in which they make their mark. Get a feel for the materials and the techniques, then evaluate the feel and emotional response to each print. In this way, you will begin to create a dialogue with your materials and the way in which you might choose to use them in the future.

Types of Stamps

Self-Adhesive Craft Foam Stamps

Craft foam can be bought as a sheet, with or without an adhesive backing attached. Of course, the adhesive backing allows you to forgo the use of glue. Craft foam can also be purchased in precut designs.

To make a self-adhesive craft foam stamp, you'll need:

* Self-adhesive craft foam
* Scissors or razor blade
* Plexiglas cut to size (see "Mounting with Plexiglas," page 23)

1. Draw the design onto the protective backing of the self-adhesive craft foam.
2. Cut out your design.
3. Peel away the protective backing and adhere the foam to the Plexiglas.

Cardboard Stamps

Corrugated cardboard creates a highly textured and fun, if short-lived, stamp. You cannot wash cardboard; instead, you'll just allow the dye (or paint) to dry on the stamp and reuse it as often as you are able to get a precise, clean print.

To make cardboard stamps, you'll need:

* Corrugated cardboard
* #11 X-acto knife

1. Draw your design directly on the cardboard.
2. Carefully cut the design, making sure you cut just the top flat linerboard. You will sometimes cut down into the fluted corrugated sheet, and this is okay. Do not cut all three layers of the cardboard.
3. Working parallel to the corrugated layer, gently lift the topmost linerboard up off the corrugated layer, leaving your cut design adhered to the corrugation.

Craft Foam

Cardboard Stamps

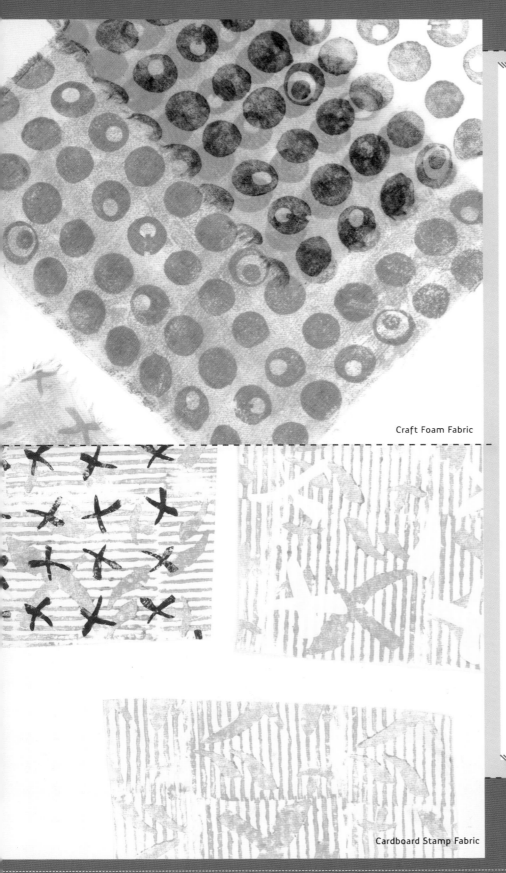

Craft Foam Fabric

Cardboard Stamp Fabric

Tie this in ...
Mounting Stamps with Plexiglas

Plexiglas is a great mount for craft foam and alternative stamp materials such as drawer liners and tile spacers. Because of its transparency, you can see through your design to the cloth you are stamping. To cut Plexiglas, you will need to hold the Plexiglas and ruler in place in order to make quick, decisive score marks with the Plexiglas cutter. Then snap the Plexiglas along the scoring. Wear goggles to protect your eyes.

To cut Plexiglas, you'll need:
- Plexiglas
- ⅛" (3 mm) thick plastic ruler
- Plexiglas cutter
- Safety goggles

1. Determine your stamp size, then plan to cut your Plexiglas about ⅛" (3 mm) bigger on all four sides.
2. Place the ruler on top of the Plexiglas.
3. Score with the Plexiglas cutter using quick, decisive strokes. You'll want a single, clean, deep score mark. This may take as many as five or six passes.
4. Place the scored Plexiglas on the edge of the table, score side up, with the score mark overhanging the table by ⅛" (3 mm).
5. Wearing your goggles, hold the Plexiglas firmly against the table and, with your other hand, snap the Plexiglas along the scored mark.
6. Repeat if needed to obtain the correct dimensions.

Soft Block Carving

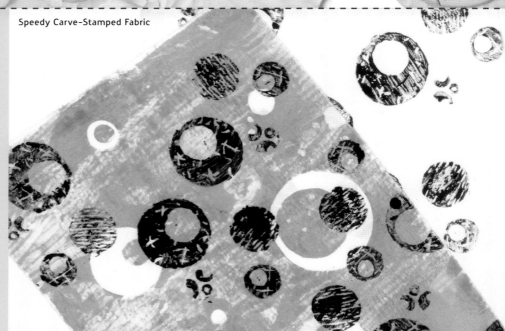
Speedy Carve-Stamped Fabric

Soft Block Carving Stamps

Carving your own stamps from rubber is the best way to get detail and intricate designs from your handmade stamps. Your designs can be as detailed as your patience allows. Over time, these stamps may become brittle and might require being mounted on a rigid surface, such as Plexiglas (see page 23).

To make soft block carving stamps, you'll need:

• Speedy Carve rubber
• #11 X-acto knife or linoleum cutters

1. Cut the Speedy Carve rubber to its final size with your X-acto knife.
2. Draw your design directly on the rubber.
3. Using the X-acto knife, cut away from your drawn line at a 45° angle and about ⅛" (3 mm) deep.
4. Carve away unwanted areas of rubber.

{ Tip Directional Designs

Remember that if your design is directional—lettering, for example—you will need to create a mirror image of the design in order for it to print properly. Copy shops can help you mirror the image. To transfer a directional design onto your stamp surface, use Saral paper, found in your local art supply store (see Resources, page 134).

Glue Stamps

Glue Stamps

Glue stamps create a look like no other stamping technique. The glue dries in unexpected ways that helps create fun and interesting prints. This is another stamp that you cannot wash. Just dry and reuse it for as long as you get a clean print.

To make glue stamps, you'll need:

♦ Cardboard
♦ Thick white craft glue, such as Aileen's

1. Draw your design directly on the cardboard.
2. Dispense glue in dots or lines; tall dots and thick lines of glue work best.
3. Allow to dry completely.

This is the one stamp that demands you use it in a different manner than a traditional stamp. For this stamp, you will apply dye to the surface of the stamp and lay the stamp, dye-side up, on your print table. Gently drape your prepared fabric on top and brayer the cloth down onto the inked stamp.

Glue Stamp Fabric

Experiment!

Don't forget stamps can be made from almost anything! Tile spacers, picture frame wall protectors, drawer liners, foam bits—you name it. Stamp making gives a trip to the hardware store a whole new meaning. Wandering the aisles looking for printable objects is a lot more fun than planning your next home improvement endeavor! If you bring the object home to find that the dye does not want to adhere to the surface and allow a clean print, add a single drop of liquid soap to your thickened dye mixture, and then print away.

Found Object Stamps

Found Object Fabric

Printing with Stamps

Now that you've learned several types of stamps to make, the real fun—printing—can start.

To print with stamps, you'll need:

* Iron
* Soda-soaked cloth (see page 19)
* Pins
* Print board
* Paint tray or cupcake tin
* Dye concentrate
* Premixed thickener
* Mixing brush
* Stamp
* White foam roller with handle (or inexpensive bristle brushes, foam brushes, or sponges)

1. Iron the soda-soaked cloth, then pin it to the print board.
2. In a paint tray, add dye concentrate to about ⅓ cup of thickener and mix thoroughly. You'll want this to be the consistency of heavy cream. It should flow off of your brush in a continuous line. Always test your color on scrap material.
3. Apply the dye to the stamp's surface with a foam roller.
4. Press the inked stamp onto the cloth.

Transferring thickened dye to the stamp can be done with any and all of the mentioned rollers and brushes. Each will give a different texture and allow you to use more or less dye. The roller will allow the least amount of dye but will cover the stamp the most evenly. Bristle brushes and sponges will leave a certain texture on the surface of the stamp. Foam brushes, when used to dab the thickened dye onto the surface of the

Found object foam stamp in combination with a craft foam stamp.

stamp, can produce the darkest application of dye, if that is your preference.

Take care when applying the dye to the stamp; globs of dye will pool along the edge of your stamp surface. Try to achieve clean and precise printing habits; keep a small brush, rag, or cotton swab nearby to clean your stamps before printing.

Prior to making that first print or mark, I suggest that you draw creative energy to you. Think of this as a creative tempest. Surround yourself with inspiration, leaf through magazines for color inspiration, visuals of other artists' work that strike a chord within you, and wander around this visual feast for a while.

At this point, too much is a good thing. Allow your mind to float, catch upon a sparkly bit, and then land on a particular thought or idea that might help you in your quest to print beautiful cloth with stamps. Try to disengage from the particulars before you and wander in the thoughts and ideas that arise from looking at and admiring the inspiration. You might even call this artistic meditation; trust the process and know that your own voice and visual needs will make themselves known to you.

Then leap, making sure you sing brightly in your own voice.

Organza, with half of freezer–paper stencil removed to show effect of both the applied freezer paper and the printed organza.

To make freezer-paper stencils, you'll need:

* Freezer paper
* X-acto knife
* Iron
* Soda-soaked cloth (see page 19)
* Paint tray
* Dye concentrate
* Premixed thickener
* Mixing brush
* Squeegee
* Rag

1. Draw your design on the freezer paper and cut it out with an X-acto knife. The design should be 2" (5 cm) narrower than your squeegee in order to get a clean print.
2. Iron the freezer paper to the soda-soaked cloth.
3. In the paint tray, add the dye concentrate to the thickener and mix thoroughly. For this technique, you'll get the best results if your dye is a tad thicker than heavy cream. Thin dye has the tendency to seep under the edge of the freezer paper.
4. Spoon a dollop of dye just above the ironed cut-out, then pull the squeegee through the dye and toward you at a 30° angle from the table.
5. Squeegee each motif separately, taking care as you go not to fold the design back on itself.
6. Do not allow pools of dye to accumulate on the freezer-paper stencil; wipe them off with a rag as you go.

Working with Freezer Paper

Freezer paper is an indispensable tool in the fiber artist's tool chest. It acts as a resist and can be used as a stencil to do impromptu screen printing, to mask out entire areas of a design, or to keep a small area of a design totally white.

Freezer paper is adhered to cloth by ironing the shiny side to the face of the cloth. It needs a high temperature and a firm hand to adhere properly, which can be a challenge to the surface design artist. Soda ash (see page 19), the fixative we use to bind dye molecules to cotton and silk, is flammable—hesitate with your iron for just one moment and a scorch mark will appear.

Be careful when ironing freezer paper to soda-soaked cloth; use quick, firm strokes.

Check the edge of the freezer paper to make sure that it is adhered around the entire edge of your freezer-paper design; otherwise, dye will creep under the edge of the freezer paper and may spoil the effect you are trying to achieve.

FREEZER-PAPER STENCILS

Freezer-paper stencils are a great and inexpensive way to practice screen printing and stenciling. A little imagination can go a long way with this valuable product. Make sure you always have a lot of freezer paper on hand for when the mood strikes.

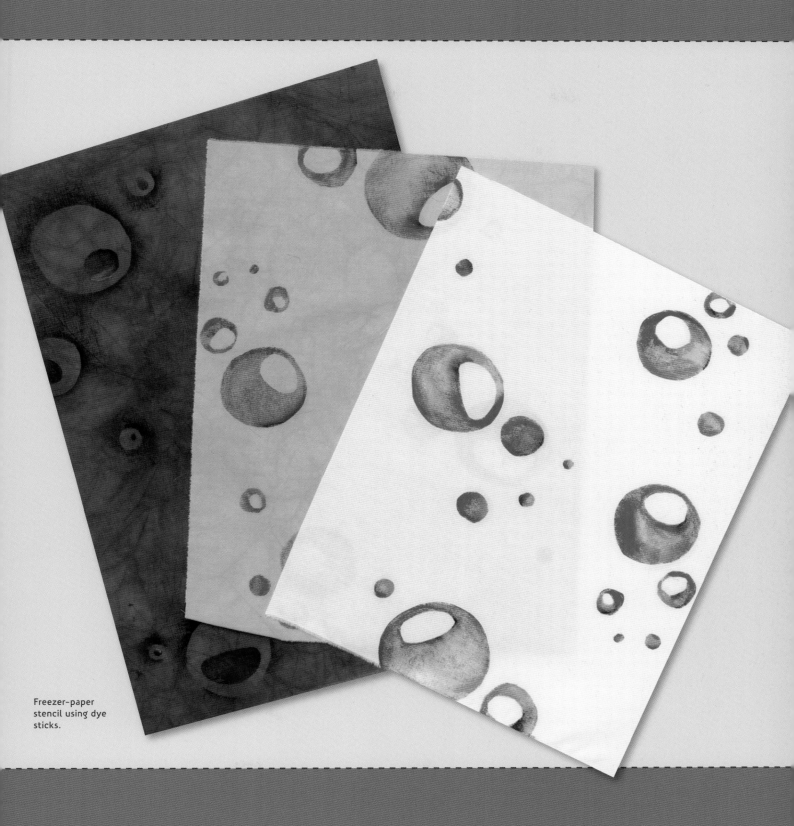

Freezer-paper
stencil using dye
sticks.

FREEZER-PAPER MASK

Using freezer paper as a mask can help you keep an area of cloth untouched, reserving it for later applications, such as direct-dye painting (see page 41). Or you can preserve textured, printed, and monoprinted areas of cloth and apply additional layers of color and texture. Masks can be as simple or as detailed as need be and can protect either the positive image (the object itself) or the negative image (the space around the object).

Play with this concept; it is the basis for creating quilt tops in two layers, which will be discussed later.

Think of these five images below as a timeline where freezer paper is applied to the cloth between each application of dye consecutively. After the final application of dye, you remove the freezer paper to reveal each previously protected color from white, through yellow (1), orange (2), red (3), and blue (4).

Fig. 1

For ease of demonstration, freezer paper was placed on monoprint ground to show negative printing (Figure 1) and also positive printing (Figure 2).

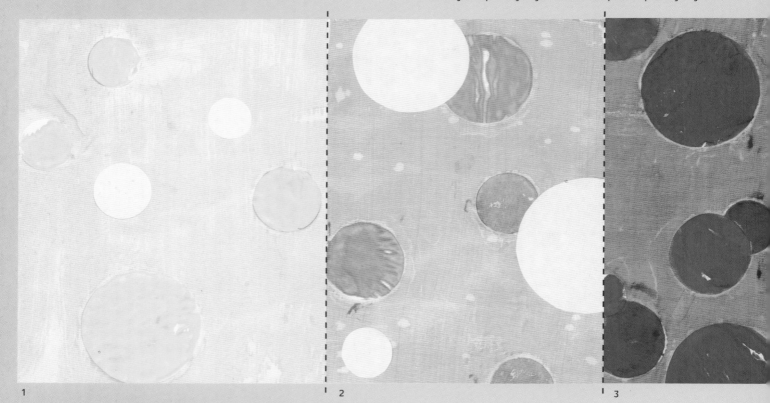

1

2

3

Fig. 2

When you begin using this technique, obviously your freezer paper will be colored and printed over before removal.

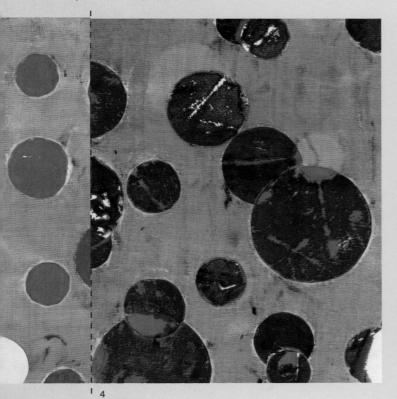

4

Final piece

Placing printed organza on top of the other fabrics will
help you understand how color changes by doing so.

To make a freezer-paper mask,
you'll need:

♦ Freezer paper
♦ Scissors
♦ Iron
♦ Soda-soaked cloth (see page 19)
♦ Dye concentrate
♦ Premixed thickener

1. Draw your design on freezer paper.
2. Cut out your design with scissors and
   iron it, shiny side down, to the soda-
   soaked cloth.
3. Now you are ready to work with
   thickened dyes. Experiment with
   monoprinting and direct-dye painting.

When using organza, place your sample
over several disparate pieces of printed
cloth and see the issue of color theory
arise. The windows of color and shade
will be affected differently on each piece
of cloth. This sample illustrates how many
color applications can be achieved and the
resulting transparency of each subsequent
layer.

Monoprinting

Monoprinting's chief characteristic is defined by the ability to make just a single print that is barely reproducible. Using Plexiglas or plastic sheeting, apply a thin layer of thickened dye, texturize it, then apply additional colors of dye with a brush or remove areas of dye until you are satisfied. Then carefully apply the prepared fabric, brayer it to ensure maximum dye transfer, and lift off the print plate.

You can create texture with combs, brushes, spatulas, cotton swabs, twigs—anything you can think of. Press stamps into the inked plate, lay torn strips of newspaper down, or apply bits of masking tape directly to your cloth and monoprint, removing the tape after the piece has dried.

You might try applying several gradations of colors and textural layers interspersed with freezer paper, doilies, lace, or leaves to create a saturated and vibrant palette. Placing a scattering of leaves (or any other flat object) between the layers of monoprinting will create windows of color and texture as well as depth of field.

Be open to what may happen. Once you lift the fabric off the plate, ghost images may remain on the plate. Play and explore! Be sure to have several ironed soda-soaked pieces of cloth ready to pick up those ghost images.

You might try utilizing monoprinting (shown in example below) to make binding material.

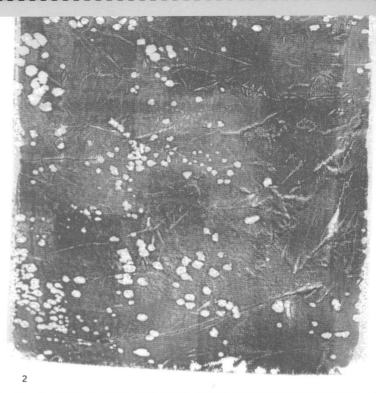

1   2

These organically shaped bubbles were obtained by having an extremely clean print surface. This set of photos also illustrates the layering of three different colors—first yellow (1), then red is applied (2), then blue (3). The bubbles act as windows to the previous layers.

To monoprint, you'll need:

- Iron
- Soda-soaked cloth (see page 19)
- Dye concentrate
- Premixed thickener
- Paint tray
- Mixing brush
- Plexiglas
- Foam roller with handle
- Texturizing materials
- Fine artist's spatula
- Masks (freezer paper, string, soy wax, leaves; be creative)
- Brayer

1. Iron the soda-soaked cloth.
2. Mix the dye and thickener in the paint tray until it is the consistency of heavy cream. It should flow off your brush in a continuous line.
3. Drizzle the mixture onto the Plexiglas sheet.
4. Using the foam roller, roll an even layer of dye just larger than your cloth.
5. Create texture with various materials, remove areas of dye with a fine spatula, and place masks on the Plexiglas or apply freezer paper to your cloth.

6. Holding the cloth taut over your print surface, drag the bottom edge toward the inked area of the plate. Lower the fabric onto the inked plate.
7. Brayer the fabric from north to south, then outward from east to west, to ensure complete dye transfer. Carefully lift off the cloth.

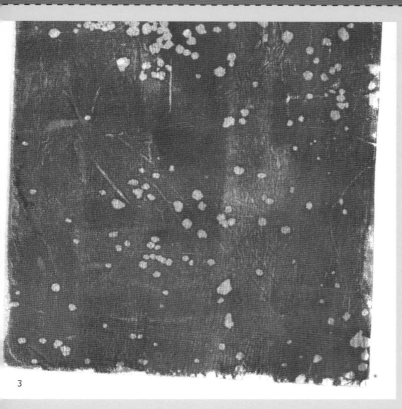

3

This texture was created by applying dye to a plate using a cheap bristle brush in straight strokes.

This texture was achieved by pressing a stamp into the inked plate, removing the stamp, and printing off the plate.

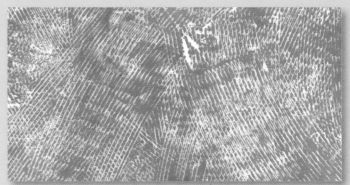

This texture was created using a faux painting rubber comb.

Tip Monoprinting with Freezer Paper

Freezer paper can be applied directly to cloth prior to monoprinting. However, it may begin to pull away from your cloth as you lift it from your print plate. To prevent this, use an artist's spatula to help lift both the fabric and the freezer paper away from the print plate. Be sure to iron the freezer paper back in place prior to further applications.

SOY WAX: A PAINTERLY RESIST

In addition to stamps, stencils, and masks, another really fun and easy way to add texture to your cloth is to use soy wax as a resist technique.

Soy wax works in the very same way as traditional paraffin wax batik, with the benefit of being able to be washed out in your home washing machine. It's a lot easier, faster, and user-friendly. Soy wax is biodegradable and has a very low melt temperature of 180°F (82°C). You will need to purchase an electric skillet with a detailed temperature gauge. The wax can be allowed to cool and harden in this pot and will be constantly at the ready.

You will need to set aside a set of bristle brushes, foam brushes, tjanting tools, and kitchen tools to be used exclusively with your wax pot (see photo at right).

Finding tools that can be used to transfer wax to cloth is exciting. Primitive kitchen tools, potato mashers, cookie molds, and snips of tin are great to use. If an object does not have a handle, a hemostatic clamp (a surgical tool that resembles needle-nosed pliers with a lockable grip) can be used as a temporary handle.

The fun and interesting part about using soy wax as a resist is in playing up the attributes of the medium to their best advantage. You might try drawing a leaf pattern in loose repeat across your cloth and direct-dye paint within the soy wax line. When the dye is dry, try painting the entire leaf pattern with wax, in effect sealing what you have already painted under a layer of wax. At this point, you can monoprint or stamp over the leaves. This technique creates textural differences that cannot be achieved by any other means.

If you want to get the traditional crackle design found on many batiked pieces, paint an entire design with soy wax (only the front is necessary), roll the fabric into a soft tube, and place it in the freezer for a while. Before you are ready to take the piece out of the freezer, mix a batch of thickened, dark-colored dye. Remove the fabric from the freezer and crumple it over a trash can. Open the fabric and pour the thickened dye in thin strands over it, then use a paint roller to push the thickened dye into the cracks in the soy wax. Batch and wash.

Soy-wax Chips

Tools for working
with soy wax.

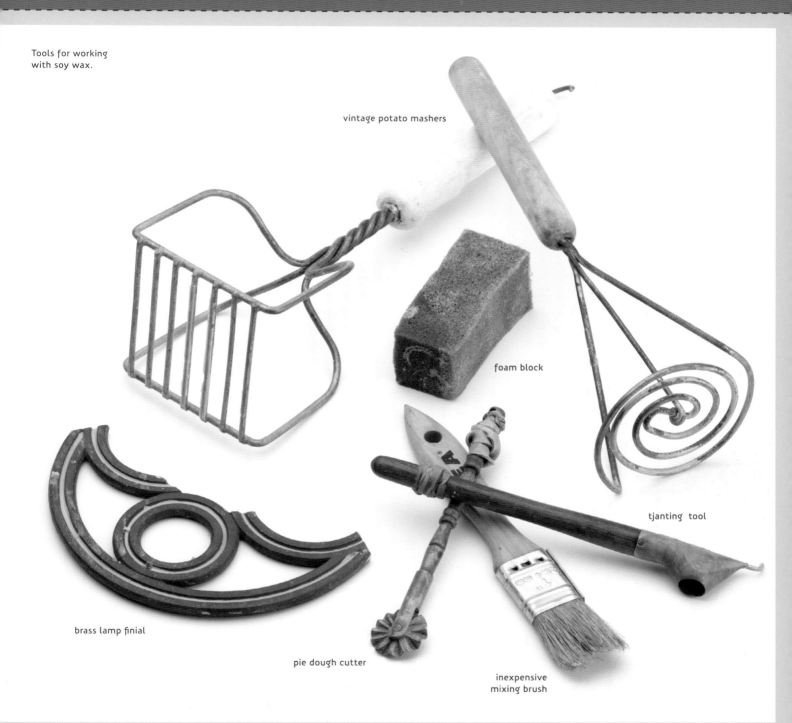

vintage potato mashers

foam block

tjanting tool

brass lamp finial

pie dough cutter

inexpensive
mixing brush

Draw the design with a tjanting tool, then dye-paint inside the soy wax "moat."

Draw lines on top of the design with an extruder.

Paint soy wax over the entire leaf motif, then monoprint the background.

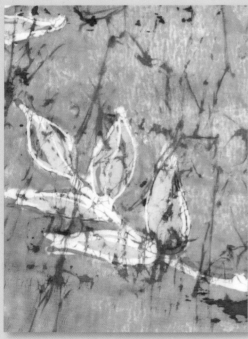

Paint soy wax over the entire surface, then freeze, crackle, and apply thickened dye with roller into the cracks.

To use soy wax, you'll need:

* Soy wax
* Electric skillet or deep fryer with adjustable temperature gauge
* Foam and bristle brushes, tjanting tools, kitchen tools
* Soda-soaked cloth (see page 19)
* Dye concentrate
* Premixed thickener
* Paint tray
* Mixing brush

1. Place the wax in the skillet and heat it to 180° to 200°F (82° to 93°C). When properly heated, the wax will appear transparent.
2. Transfer the wax from pot to the cloth. When done properly, the wax will sink into and through the cloth.
3. Combine the dye concentrate and thickener in a paint tray. Dye-paint into, monoprint over, apply more wax, and then more dye!

The example at right is a monoprinted broadcloth. It was monoprinted orange and then a foam block was used as a stamp to transfer soy wax (1). Finally, a foam roller was used to push dye into the remaining surface of cloth (2). The completed piece is shown (3).

{

Tip **Using Soy Wax Successfully**
A metal lid can help you transfer wax from the pot to your fabric without dripping the wax in unintended places. You can reuse the wax accumulated in the lid, allow it to harden, and twist the lid over the wax pot. Remember that wax is hot and should not be left unattended.

1. Orange monoprinted broadcloth, foam block used as a stamp to transfer soy wax to cloth.

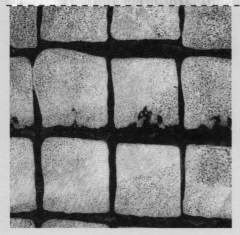

2. Drizzle a dark color over the soy-waxed surface and use a foam roller to push dye into the cracks.

3. Completed cloth.

A map or pattern for direct-dye painting.

Direct-Dye Painting

Painting dye directly onto cloth can be extremely satisfying. Quick strokes of color or practiced drawings can take on a life of their own. Brushes—both foam and bristle—squeeze-top bottles and extruders are just the tip of the iceberg when applying dye to cloth.

Let's talk about paintbrushes. Every type of brush has its use: cheap hardware store brushes can give a piece great texture but won't allow for fine or detailed work, unless you choose to work on a large scale. Foam brushes are also quite useful because they can hold a great deal of dye. They have their place next to an artist's palette, too.

The real joy in painting comes from a good brush! Luckily for us, dye is very similar to watercolor paint, so watercolor brushes work well with this medium. Watercolor brushes come in a variety of shapes and descriptive designations, including round, flat, fan, and filbert, to name a few. Over time and with practice, you will learn to exploit the intent of each style of brush; you will even be able to make a fine line while using, say, a number 8 round. It is also useful to use a brush appropriate to the size of your work; large areas require large brushes. More often than not, I reach for a size 1, 3, or 6 round watercolor brush or a ½" or 1" (1.3 or 2.5 cm) flat.

I encourage you to experiment, play, and relax with painting. Try working with dry brush techniques. This is an easy technique when painting on cloth because cloth has tooth and resistance and wants to accept dye from a brush in a scratchy effect, which is the definition of dry brush. Then try working wet on wet. Mix several colors of dye, load half your brush with one color and half with the other, and see what happens. Try leaving a thick edge of thickened dye and painting into it with another color. Each application will give different results, and you will gain experience in trying them out.

A good set of watercolor brushes are an investment. Do not allow them to sit in a cup of water, and do your best not to allow dye or paint to get up into the ferrule (the metal area that acts as a clamp to adhere the bristles to the handle). It is best to load your brush to within ⅛" (3 mm) of the ferrule. And do not allow paint or dye to dry on the bristles of the brush. Following these simple rules will prolong the life of the brush.

PAINTING INTO A PREVIOUSLY PROTECTED AREA

Try using this technique in conjunction with freezer-paper masks (see page 30) to paint into an area previously protected by freezer paper. To narrow the field of possibility, create a predetermined palette of a limited number of colors. When mixing the colors, use a test piece of fabric to see whether the mixed colors play well. Get into the habit of working from light to dark because it is easier to fix mistakes this way (you can easily put brown over yellow, but not yellow over brown).

You may want to take the guesswork out of the painting process altogether and plot out the light, medium, and dark areas of your intended painting. Place this sketch under a piece of plastic sheeting, tape your cloth to the plastic sheeting, and proceed.

Tip Buy a Good Brush

When purchasing brushes, test them by dipping them into a cup of water; high-quality stores will provide this. Once you have dipped the brush in water, drag the wet brush across the tip of your finger. A great watercolor brush will provide tactile resistance and snap back to a perfect point.

Fig. 1

Try leaving small areas unpainted. White can create fabulous areas that "pop" off the artwork.

White can also overwhelm a piece; learning a pleasing balance is essential. Your eye should float over the piece and not be irresistibly drawn to a single unbalanced spot.

To paint into a previously protected area, you'll need:

* Premixed thickener
* Concentrated dye
* Design
* Plastic sheeting
* Tape
* Soda-soaked cloth (see page 19)
* Round watercolor brushes

1. Create a limited palette of colors that work well together (Figure 1).
2. Place the design under the plastic sheeting.
3. Tape the cloth to the plastic sheeting.
4. Working from light to dark, begin painting, following your design.

This process takes practice. To blend colors you might try placing a "bead" of dye in its intended spot. Stock your brush with the color you would like to blend and drag your brush through the bead of dye, applying both colors in one stroke. This is called working wet on wet. An example of this is where the gray meets the brown (Figure 2).

The gray dye accents the bird's feathers, separating and dividing them, and creates an area of darker contrast.

In Figure 3, the colors were not worked wet on wet; instead, the gray was applied first, and then the brown. This is why the gray appears darker. It did not blend—as a result, it maintained its saturation.

Figure 4 shows the painting of the darkest color (brown). In this example, the eye could make or break the image. Painting the eye correctly will elevate the image. Conversely, if your hand is not steady and the eye is painted improperly, it will ruin the image. This is because eyes are a point of connection with the viewer. Not only will viewers connect with that part of the image first, but they'll also be able to discern the tiniest discrepancy. Learn to understand which parts of an image are

most important. Then steady your hand, and paint that area with extra care.

Your skills will develop with practice. Being an artist is essentially akin to being a researcher. It is imperative to gather inspiration, photographs, and background information on your chosen subject. This bird is a shrike, a passerine, or a songbird that uses tools, such as barbed wire, to kill its prey and was originally photographed for the pages of a favorite birding magazine. Upon receiving the magazine, I sat and did a meticulous crosshatch-style drawing based on the photograph in my journal. When finished, I read the accompanying article, increasing both my visual and my intellectual knowledge of the subject.

Since then, I have re-created this image multiple times in several compositions. Each time, I take out my drawing and the inspirational photograph. The more you work with a single image, the better you will become at interpreting it. With each interpretation, you will notice something new, such as slight variations in color that you hadn't seen before or a line or an angle that could push the drawing to a higher level. Immerse yourself!

Fig. 2

Fig. 3

Fig. 4

THICK-AND-THIN LINE PAINTING

Creating a thick-and-thin line is a dramatic means of applying a hand-drawn look to cloth. It takes a little bit of practice to apply fluid lines. Always keep a scrap piece of cloth nearby to test your hand prior to starting in on your final piece; your painting style will change from day to day and according to mood.

A thick-and-thin line is attainted by initially using just the tip of your brush, then bearing down to use the midsection, and again retreating to the tip of the brush. This creates a line that is at first thin, then thick, then thin again—just as the name of the technique implies. I especially like using this application on organza, because the effect is quite striking.

The sampler below shows various brushstrokes.

1. 2" (5 cm) foam brush fading to dry brush effect
2. ½" (1.3 cm) cheap bristle brush fading to dry brush effect
3. 1½" (4 cm) cheap bristle brush fading to dry brush effect
4. Size 0 round watercolor brush thick-and-thin line
5. Size 2 round watercolor brush thick-and-thin line
6. Size 4 round watercolor brush thick-and-thin line
7. Size 6 round watercolor brush thick-and-thin line
8. Size 8 round watercolor brush thick-and-thin line
9. ½" (1.3 cm) square at 90°
10. 1" (2.5 cm) square at 90°
11. ½" (1.3 cm) square fading to dry brush effect
12. 1" (2.5 cm) square fading to dry brush effect

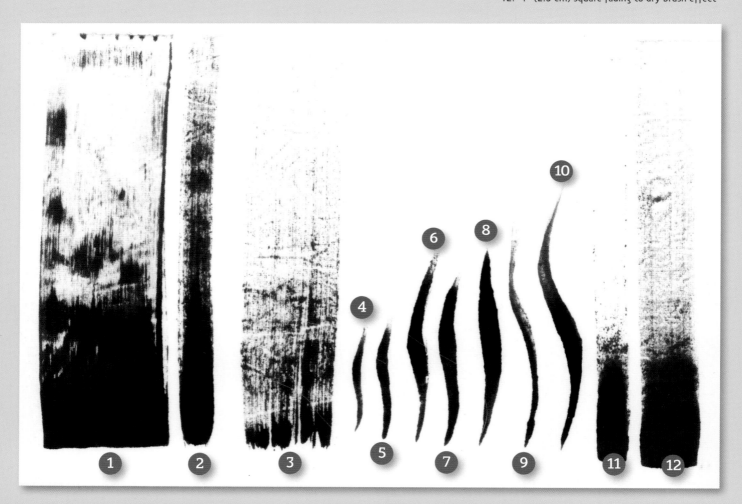

To create a thick-and-thin line, you'll need:

• Design
• Plastic sheeting
• Masking tape
• Soda-soaked cloth (see page 19)
• Premixed thickener
• Concentrated dye
• Paint tray
• Watercolor brushes

1. Place the design under plastic sheeting, and tape the cloth on top of the plastic.
2. Mix the thickener and dye in a paint tray.
3. Using a round watercolor brush, apply the dye, varying the pressure you use to apply the thick-and-thin line **(Figure 1)**.

This chapter could stand alone and be a book in itself. The material presented here has only laid the foundation for an approach to making whole-cloth quilts. I encourage you to use this chapter as a workbook. Methodically play with the ideas presented, keep notes, and preserve some of your samples in your three-ring binder. The only way to gain experience and become fully grounded in any technique is to get dirty, make mistakes, have success, and play. Allow yourself to loosen up and expand.

In the next chapter, you'll learn how to create a whole-cloth quilt in two layers. I will show you how to create a map, make lists of techniques that might express the idea, register the fabrics, and use them to their best advantage.

Experiment!

Cotton broadcloth and silk organza will accept dye differently. I suggest you make a sampler of each type of brushstroke described (see example on page 44) and place these samples in your binder for future reference.

Fig. 1

Let's expand the explorations of Chapter 2 by creating whole-cloth quilt tops painted once on cotton broadcloth and again on silk organza, mixing, matching, and layering the techniques learned. The beauty of layering silk organza atop cotton broadcloth lies in the properties of the sheer organza. When organza has been painted, textured, resisted, and painted into, then placed on top of the cotton, which has also been painted and textured, the color and depth of the two pieces together strengthen the overall effect of the fabric. The sheer organza allows collaged elements to be placed between these two printed layers, making commercial or hand-printed cloth sing. Painted textures on the organza lend a painterly effect to these prints, unifying and integrating the whole.

Kind, 16" × 14¼" (40.5 × 36 cm). Organza: Freezer-paper-resist bird, dogwood, petals, letter Os, mono-print, thick-and-thin line, direct-dye paint petals. Broadcloth: Freezer-pa-per-resist dogwood, monoprint, freezer-paper screenprint yellow dots. Collage, gradation machine-quilting and embroidery.

Finding Your Visual Language

There is an element of trust in creating work in this manner. Some of the design elements are defined by the dye paint, freezer-paper resists, soy wax, or stamping techniques. Others can be completed using your own cloth or commercial prints. Befriend this feeling of artistic ambiguity, knowing that you can and will find solutions that dance, shimmer, and resonate. It is also important to keep in mind that almost any misstep in printing can be fixed, embellished upon, or hidden.

I will draw upon imagery from my own journals while at the same time offering exercises to expand and deepen your own journaling explorations. Maintaining a journal is a holistic exercise; it allows you quick and easy access to your own internal creative world, and given time, your own personal visual language will emerge and exert itself (which is the ultimate goal of being an artist). The interplay between the journal page and your approach to creating works on cloth will develop and intensify when you just stick with the process.

Experiment!

A fun way to begin using paint and to gain an understanding of color is to place a piece of tracing paper over a page of a magazine. Mix similar colors to what you see through the tracing paper and "trace paint." Don't be meticulous—place colors quickly and assuredly. Block color and its placement out, then analyze why it works and why the colors were used in that manner to begin with. These quick trace paintings can be glued into your journals and doodled over. Have fun, relax, and explore.

This map shows a general direction for the piece that became *Kind* (see page 46). Dark marker suggests thick-and-thin lines. Shading within the dogwood flowers reminds me to paint there.

Making a Map

The map is an overall plan to direct and guide each work of art. A map helps focus the intent of the artwork you plan to create. Calling it a map reminds us to be flexible. Side trips can be taken. Most times, creating art is about the journey, not necessarily the destination. A map can also be considered a way in which to guide your thoughts and does not need to be strictly adhered to, as the use of the word pattern might. The main elements in your map should be drawn out in marker; all else can be worked in pencil to be penned when committed to.

To make a map, you'll need:

* Tape
* Paper slightly larger than proposed work
* Projector
* Journal with lots of images
* Pens and pencils

1. Tape a large piece of paper to a wall, project an image onto it, and find a pleasing size.
2. Trace the image.
3. Assess the image and make notes.

The drawn aspect of the finished work will only be as good as this map. Make sure your drawing is satisfactory; correct any missteps now.

When assessing your map, it's good to ask yourself some questions. For example:
* Which part of the image should remain white right now?
* Will shading (called "painting into," see page 41) benefit this image?
* Which techniques will fulfill my vision?
* Which parts of the image can be addressed when progressing on to collage?

At this point, the possibilities of a piece are endless; you've barely even begun! Because of this, I think this is a great time to sort through stamps, page through three-ring binders, look for color combinations, and call inspiration to the forefront of possibility. The goal is to stimulate your creative center and allow an opening for new ideas and approaches. Gathering inspiration feeds your inner artist. Do not allow yourself to work in a vacuum!

Working in this manner will help solidify your intent in creating the piece. At the same time, you will find that once you start working, the piece will begin to have a mind of its own, and some of the ideas you had gathered around you will fall to the wayside; this is part of the process and can be magical.

Experiment!

This will be a conceptual experiment. Make a three-column list (see below). In the first column, list techniques you feel comfortable using. In the second column, write a list of rules you feel are needed to obtain good results with each technique listed in the previous column. In the third column, think up ways to break those rules.

For example, prior to writing this book I believed that I could not obtain fine detail when using freezer paper as a resist. Then I made *Yellowstone Chair* (see above), which has a caned back fine detail, and I was able to monoprint and maintain precise lines in printing, and my preconceived ideas about obtaining good results with freezer-paper masks were forever changed. This led me to create *Country Chair* and *City Chair* (whose chairs are less than 1" (2.5 cm) tall; see right), and all three blew my old beliefs out of the water. Break your own rules; break mine, for that matter.

My three columns would look like this:

Yellowstone Chair, 5" × 8½" (13 x 22.5 cm).

City Chair, 5" × 8" (12.5 x 20 cm).

Country Chair, 5" × 8" (12.5 x 20 cm).

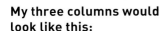

Freezer-paper masks

This technique requires broad areas of coverage and a firm hand when ironing so no seepage will occur.

Why not try an intricate design? Try a small piece that can easily be discarded if adverse printing occurs.

Registering the Layers

Now we will begin creating whole-cloth works on two layers—silk organza and cotton broadcloth. Organza is an inherently transparent fabric and will always be the topmost layer. The cotton layer becomes the base or foundation. Together, the two will support one another and help each other shine. Cutting a set of freezer-paper masks and registering the image first on the cotton, then on the organza, is the best way to keep an area of cloth white and provides a solid starting point. Registering the two masks is an easy process.

REGISTERING THE MASKS

You may need to tape several widths of freezer paper together in order to completely mask out your design. If this is the case, overlap the freezer paper by a ½" (1.3 cm) and secure in several places with masking tape, which withstands ironing better than transparent tape does.

Remember to cut two freezer-paper masks, one for the organza and another for the cotton.

To register the masks:

1. Cut two sets of freezer paper to the desired height and prepare them for the correct width.
2. Using your map, trace the design onto a sheet of freezer paper.
3. Place the tracing on top of the second prepared sheet of freezer paper, shiny side down, and staple them together, making sure you staple outside your drawn line.

4. Cut out the freezer-paper mask.
5. While remaining aware of the grain of the cloth, apply the first freezer-paper mask to soda-soaked cotton (see page 19), ironing at a temperature just below the cotton setting. Remember to use quick, firm strokes to avoid scorching. Leave the cloth on the ironing board.
6. Center the organza over the broadcloth layer.
7. Register the placement of the second freezer-paper mask against the ironed cotton below. Iron the second freezer-paper mask onto the organza.

The goal of the freezer-paper mask is that it remains in place on the fabric it is adhered to throughout the printing process, or until you decide otherwise. As you monoprint, stamp, and apply more and more dye to the cloth, this mask will begin to pull away. Allow the fabric to dry between applications and iron the mask into place before proceeding with subsequent layers.

Silk organza tends to shrink by about 6 percent, so remember to cut your organza slightly larger than your broadcloth or learn to love the raw edge.

Experiment!

Using images in the public domain or perhaps your own photographs, trace the outline of an image that speaks to you. Take this tracing and paint around the drawn image, directly on the tracing paper. Be free with the paint, smoosh one color into another, and allow yourself to see "what happens if. . . ." Allow to dry.

Play with this bit of tracing paper. Place it over a page in your journal or a page of a magazine. Flip it over to see how it looks paint side down. The unpainted area will allow images below to show through. When this piece "finds a home," glue it down using a glue stick. It is best to apply the glue to the more stable of the two papers you are trying to adhere together. If the tracing paper needs to be trimmed, allow it to dry and carefully tear away unwanted areas.

I enlarged a photograph of my cat for this exercise.

Journal inspiration for *Kind* (see page 46). Gouache, tracing-paper painting (bird), stamped, and painted.

Layering and Transparency

This is where the fun begins. Any and all of the techniques explored in Chapter 2 can be used to create your design. You will create the same image twice—once on the cotton and again on the organza, always keeping color theory in mind. The organza layer will affect the color of the cotton layer below. Always work from light to dark. You can apply red on top of yellow, but it is difficult to see the effects of placing yellow on top of red. Allowing the piece to dry between applications will enable you to check your color (by placing the dry organza on top of the dry broadcloth). Be methodical and work with intention.

After creating the map of the image, make notes for yourself. Ask yourself what is happening in the image you want to create. Perhaps the bird should be freezer-paper resisted on just the organza layer,

allowing the printed broadcloth to show through. Do you intend to paint a thick and thin line? Which techniques will help you bring the image to life?

Your list might look like this:
- The flower needs resist on both the cotton and the organza layers; the bird can be resisted on just the organza layer.
- The dogwood flower needs to be direct-dye painted/shaded on the organza layer after the two layers have been printed to satisfaction.
- The bird needs a thick and thin line on the organza layer.
- The leaves, branch, word banner, and letter Os can be delineated in cloth as collaged elements later.

I have outlined the exact steps taken to create the piece called *Kind* (see page 46),

but it is my hope that new creative pathways for combining these techniques will illuminate your own visual works of art.

Utilizing your notes, begin to prepare your layers for printing.
1. Apply freezer-paper masks to both cotton and silk organza **(Figures 1 and 2)**.
Starting with the silk organza:
2. Yellow monoprint **(Figure 3)**.
3. Apply freezer-paper circles near tail; monoprint blue-green **(Figure 4)**.

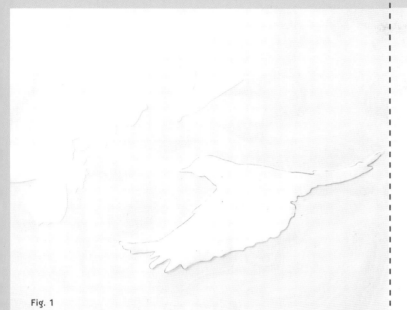

Fig. 1

Fig. 2

Fig. 3

Fig. 4

4. Remove freezer paper.
5. Paint thick-and-thin line to bird on the organza layer **(Figure 5)**.
6. Paint light pink into the dogwood petals.
7. Move to the cotton layer:
8. Monoprint a light-colored texture **(Figure 6)**.
9. Freezer-paper stencil additional design element.
10. Remove freezer paper **(Figure 7)**.
11. Apply thick-and-thin line to dogwood petals **(Figure 8)**.

As you can see, there is an ebb and flow between the two layers. As you wait for one layer to dry, you can work on the other layer. You need not wait for the piece to dry at all; wet-on-wet applications can be quite stunning. Soy-wax applications are the exception. For the wax to truly penetrate the cloth, it is best to dry your work entirely before applying the wax (see page 36).

Fig. 5

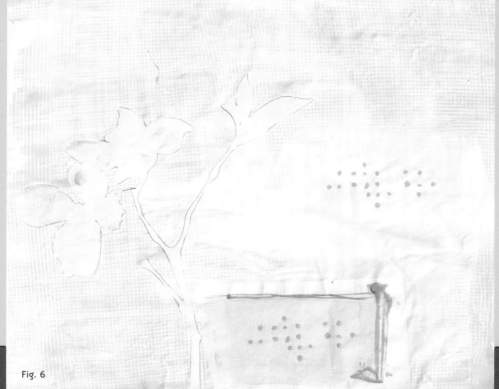

Fig. 6

Fig. 7

Fig. 8

Kind, 16" × 14¼"
(40.5 × 36 cm).

Another idea might be to use actual leaves instead of the freezer paper as a resist for the circles (Step 3, page 50). Or step out of your comfort zone and try laying string on your inked Plexiglas to create a grass-like texture. Use doilies to create stylized flowers, or perhaps your bird might need further enhancement by direct-dye painting in realistic colors. There is no right and wrong, only better and better creative explorations.

Before washing the two layers, place the organza on top of the cotton and assess your composition by asking yourself the following questions:

Does my eye settle on a specific area, and is that a good thing? If I am not happy with the results, can I change it?

Is there a good balance of light and dark areas?

Does this feel finished? Or at least finished enough to move on to collage and sewing?

Batch (see page 19) for at least 24 hours and daydream about collage and sewing. Wash, dry, and iron your whole-cloth layers and you will be ready to actualize those daydreams!

Creating Collage

I like to think of collage as my opportunity to fully embrace the decorative, or even, ornamental elements of a design. In the fine-art world, decorative art is sometimes looked down upon. Pshaw! Explore the artwork of Matisse, Klimt, Mucha, and Morris, to name just a few; this will both enforce a sense of place within the art world and justify its further use. Don't forget, textiles are firmly rooted in this category, so why not push the medium to the limits of possibility? Using collage to add a design in a loose repeat or contribute sparkling bits of color to your artwork can be quite thrilling!

Once you have batched, washed, and ironed your broadcloth and organza layers, you are ready to take the leap and embrace the decorative elements of the design process. This step is magical. It allows you to complete the mapped design elements and introduce new fabrics, textures, and motifs. It is the difference between the collaged fabrics and the dyed work that creates a feeling of substance and depth.

Sandwiching your quilt top with batting and a backing creates a firm foundation for a machine-drawn line, fusing the mapped imagery and adding a few new motifs, too. I have quite a bit of fun in this stage of the process. I use both cotton fabrics (think opaque) and silk organza (transparent) when creating collaged elements because both have their place in the overall design and each lends a different effect.

The collaged elements can be as detailed as time permits; scrollwork, text, ditties … are all fair game. Think of collage as your opportunity to continue to add visual interest or noise. As you place your collaged bits, be sure to evaluate the manner in which your eye travels the piece. You don't want your eye to get stuck. If you are unsure whether the piece flows well, pin it to your design wall upside down and view the piece from afar. This helps your mind disassociate from the content of the piece and will help you find blank spots more easily.

This is an opportunity to use your doodles and make marks. Yes, there will be some collaged elements that will need to be completed to fulfill the basic tenets of the piece, but use this as an excuse to consult your journals, your doodles, and the designs that come up with frequency when you are not even trying to draw!

Missteps in printing can be fixed at this point, too. You might be able to find a sheer fabric that blends into your pattern so perfectly that no one will notice its placement, or you might create a pretty "butterfly" to cover a wayward splotch.

Tip Rules

There is just one rule! If you want to paint a thick-and-thin line, it is best to do so only on a single layer—either the cotton or the organza—not both. Registering a set of thick-and-thin painted lines is nearly impossible.

Map for *Guardians of Being*.

Fixing Mistakes

Fixing the missteps and blunders of exuberant printing is much easier than it might first appear. As an artist (and human), it is helpful to disengage from the fear of making mistakes, because, frankly, mistakes are an opportunity to expand and think creatively. Let your mind wander, knowing that you will find a workable solution.

Often, fixes merely fool the eye away from settling on the misstep. Registering the layers can be problematic. The freezer-paper resist may not have been applied to the organza on grain, and it will only show up after the fabric has been washed, and you are about to sandwich the work and move on to the exciting part.

Never fear. Perhaps you can add a fused doodle over the wayward splotch*, add a similarly colored or textured organza between the layers, masking the cotton layer below it, or cut away the bit of organza that offends and quilt all the layers together, quickly!

In the example above, the partially inverted word Dreamlan(d) registered improperly. The organza wasn't on grain when I adhered the freezer-paper resist. After printing both layers and washing, the layers did not match up. No amount of tugging would make the letters register.

The piece required applying fusible web to some white silk habutai, a lightweight silk that is just opaque enough to cover over the "l," "a," and "n" that were misprinted, and apply it to the cotton layer.

When fixing this type of misprint, the organza layer becomes the master (map):

1. Pin the organza layer in place.
2. Lift the organza enough that you can place the fused habutai, aligning it with the organza while applying it to the cotton layer.
3. Iron the fused habutai in place.

*Bluebird is one such "fix." The "Q" of the bird's body fixes a mistake in printing.

Far left: Before silk habutai has been applied.
Near left: After silk habutai has been applied.

Detail of *Guardians of Being.* Organza: Freezer-paper-resist inverted word "Dreamlan(d)," monoprint, thick-and-thin line. Broadcloth: Freezer-paper-resist inverted word "Dreamlan(d)," soy-wax circle and lines, monoprint. Collage, tracing-paper drawing. *Note:* For the finished piece, I chose to reverse the direction of the birds' heads.

Bluebird, 11" × 10" (28 × 25.5 cm), The "Q" on the bird's belly is a "butterfly" that covers a misstep in printing. Organza: Freezer-paper-resist bird and ginkgo leaves, monoprint, direct-dye paint bird. Broadcloth: Freezer-paper-resist bird, monoprint. Collage, tracing-paper drawing, machine embroidery, machine quilting, hand embroidery, and whipstitched binding.

I find it easiest to begin the quilt sandwich at this point, but for the following two techniques (sandwiching and using synthetic sheers) you will not pin the organza layer in place (see page 63). The batting gives the work body, which is especially helpful with "synthetic demands," and holding the organza layer aside will allow you to fuse collaged elements as well as apply the synthetic sheers if you choose to do so.

Fusible Web

Fusible web is the equivalent of glue for the fiber artist. It comes adhered to a protective backing and, once heated between two layers of cloth, serves to bind them together. Luckily, the paper backing allows us to first apply the glue to the fabric we intend to adhere, cut out the design, and peel the backing away before affixing the cutout to our work of art.

This map helps to plot, cut, and place fused imagery.

Fig. 1

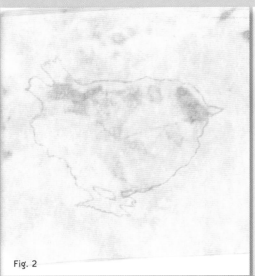

Fig. 2

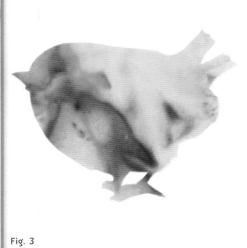

Fig. 3

Fig. 4

Fig. 5

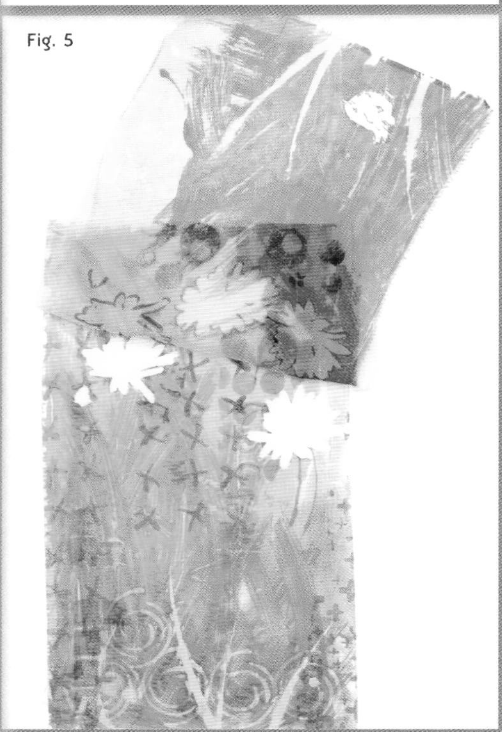

Fig. 6

Wren's Walk, 12¾" × 21½" (32.5 × 54.5 cm). Organza: Freezer-paper-resist daisies, wren, and grass, monoprint, thick-and-thin line. Broadcloth: Freezer-paper-resist daisies, wren, and grass, soy wax, monoprint, stamp. Collage, machine quilting, ⅛" (3 mm). French binding dyed to match.

To use fusible web:

1. Leaving the glue adhered to the protective backing, place the fusible web glue side up on your map. Trace with a ballpoint pen directly onto the glue. Your pen may snag on the glue; be gentle **(Figure 1)**.
2. Adhere this to the side of the cloth you intend to glue down with an iron. Peel away the backing **(Figure 2)**. *Note: Follow the manufacturer's directions for the iron temperature of your chosen fusible web.*
3. You will be able to see the traced line through the protective backing. Cut out the design just inside the drawn line to eliminate the pen mark **(Figure 3)**.
4. Using the organza layer as the map, pin the organza to the broadcloth layer in such a way as to be able to lift it gently away to place the fused elements between the two layers **(Figures 4, 5, 6)**.
5. Iron.
6. You are ready to baste all four layers together (see page 67).

Experiment!

Using text in collage can be very effective. You don't need to restrict yourself to your native tongue either! You can find online translation sites that will help you change your text from English to another language. You can also find fabulous free fonts to install on your computer. Good fonts to use in a collage have body and are bold, and they can range from traditional to script in style. Once you find the right words and font, project or enlarge the text to a size suitable for your intended piece. This can then be traced onto fusible web, applied to the fabric of your choice, and cut. Cutting out text may seem tedious, but the final effect is delicious. Try cutting text from both fused organza and broadcloth.

Synthetic sheers have a tendency to pull away from your sewn line. Because of this, I usually apply the synthetic sheer between the cotton and organza layers. Additionally, it is best to sew the synthetic sheer design from the back of the work.

To apply synthetic sheer:

1. Sandwich the broadcloth layer with your batting and backing to give the machine appliqué body. The organza layer will be added later.
2. Place your synthetic sheer on your work surface.
3. Place your partial sandwich, facedown, on top of the sheer.
4. Pin your tracing, in the proper orientation, to the back of the work. Sew through all layers, tying off as you go.
5. Tear away the tracing paper.
6. Using sharp, pointy embroidery scissors, cut away the excess synthetic sheer as close as 1/8" (3 mm) from your sewn line.
7. Using a heated soldering iron, gently melt the outermost edge of the synthetic sheer, creating a beaded line that acts as a barrier and prevents the sheer from pulling away from the stitched line.
8. You are ready to baste all four layers together (see page 67).

The most important areas to sear are on the bias in intricate areas (where hardly any cloth remains) and any areas you know will be left unprotected by your topmost layer of organza.

You are now ready to start sandwiching and quilting!

Some colors may be too dark to use this method. When this is the case, follow Step 3. Then flip the fusible web, glue side down, and trace the design once again onto the protective backing, then continue on to Step 4.

Working with Synthetic Sheers

Using machine appliqué with synthetic sheer is a fabulous way to add additional color, texture, and motifs to your design. Synthetic sheers come in such a wide range of colors and textures that it is difficult to resist the impulse to use them. Synthetic sheers can be found in gradations, tie-dyed, polka-dotted, and with metallic threads intertwined, all lending their own traits to your finished work, and there is the added benefit of being able to see through them.

Because of the low-melt temperature of most synthetics, I hesitate to use fusible web with this versatile fabric. Instead, I machine appliqué and cut away excess fabric with a combination of scissors work and melting with a soldering iron. Using scissors creates a crisp, clean line. Going back into your hand-cut lines with a soldering iron creates a fused line that prevents the synthetic sheer from pulling away from the machine appliqué, adding extra protection.

Fiore, 21" × 18½" (53.5 × 47 cm). Organza: Freezer-paper-resist bird, monoprint. Broadcloth: Positive freezer-paper-resist bird and stylized flowers, monoprint, stamp, freezer-paper-stencil Xs, negative freezer-paper-resist background, soy wax, monoprint bird. Collage and synthetic machine appliqué, tulle to darken upper left.

Daisies, 8½" × 6" (21.5 × 15 cm). Organza: Freezer-paper-resist right profile of daisy, monoprint orange, freezer-paper-resist left profile of daisy, monoprint blue. Broadcloth: Freezer-paper-resist right profile of daisy monoprint orange, freezer-paper-resist left profile of drawing, monoprint blue, stamp, machine-drawn line, whip-stitched binding.

Sandwiching the artwork to the batting and backing prior to quilting is a simple process. The one factor that is slightly different in the approach I am about to discuss is the nature of the top two layers. You will want to ensure that the organza lies properly atop the cotton layer and that the main or most important motif in the piece is secured first. Although we have been taught to safety pin the layers together from the middle out for basting, this approach isn't always best when working in the whole-cloth manner.

Sandwich and Pin

When layering organza on top of broadcloth, you will want your beautiful printing to show to its best advantage. If your organza layer shifts out of registration and is permanently fixed in that position by quilting, it may ruin your intended effect. Pinning your main motif first, and with care, ensures that no shifting will occur.

It is exciting to get to this stage in the quilting process. The tendency could be to sandwich and then quilt. I like to take it slower. Because I encourage you to assess and reevaluate as you proceed, I ask that you be flexible in this part of the process and allow for deviations and new ideas to emerge.

To begin sandwiching and pinning:

1. Cut the backing and batting 1" (2.5 cm) larger than the quilt tops. This allows for shrinkage from stitching.
2. Lay the backing fabric facedown.
3. Place the batting atop the backing.
4. Center the cotton broadcloth layer on top of the batting, faceup.
5. Place the organza on top of the broadcloth layer, aligning the major motifs.
6. Pin around the most important motif first, ensuring that no two pins are farther than 6" (15 cm) apart. As a general rule, I use straight pins on works smaller than 18" (46 cm) square and safety pins on anything larger than 18" (46 cm) square.
7. In a starburst-like manner, continue to pin outward from this area.

My motto and general approach to life and art: More IS More!

As I said, any other quilt artist would think it is time to start quilting after a quilt has been basted—but no! This is not a rule that applies here (what, you thought there were rules?). I encourage you to continually question and evaluate your design. Imagine that you are a friend, and you are critiquing the piece before you. You are not allowed to use the word nice, and if you have done your job well, the color you have used in printing the piece will draw you into the work. Color always wins the day in art; it transports and pushes the viewer to explore and experience the piece further.

So we have gotten to the point of critique. Have you, up to this point, fulfilled your vision for the piece? What could you do to push the piece beyond your wildest imagination? How can you break your own rules and preconceived ideas? In quilting this piece, can you use colored thread to push the color to another level? What is missing? Think about this process as a call and response; listen, intuit, and be present. Allow your artwork to talk back!

This is about filling in holes in your design, creating further layers of depth, and applying even more design elements. Tracing-paper drawings can be done before you begin quilting, giving you the opportunity to sew up to—but not over—your machine drawing. Conversely, you might want to place a machine-drawn line on top of the completely quilted artwork, using a contrasting thread. If you think your design is too dark, try sewing some ditties in place prior to quilting so that you can cut away the organza layer later in the process, revealing the printed cotton layer and adding both sizzle and pop to the design.

Fig. 1A

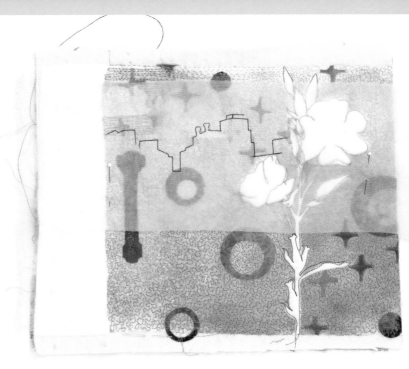

Fig. 1B

There is both give and take in allowing yourself to create artwork in this manner. There is a sense of freedom because you can change course, add new motifs, and tuck additional printed motifs between the layers. Allow this freedom to occur, have confidence in your intuition, and proceed blithely!

Tracing-Paper Drawing

Adding hand-drawn motifs before you truly begin free-motion quilting will elevate the design as a whole, allowing you to create transparent effects. This is achieved by varying the density of the free-motion machine quilting, adding tulle, cutting away the organza layer, or choosing a different quilting thread. Your choice of thread color can add a colorful kick (see the vine in *Starry, Starry Bird,* page 71). The idea is to create visual depth, as though you are looking into a stand of dominoes just before the first is tipped over and the entire design collapses. After machine quilting around the machine-drawn lines, the areas that do not have quilting will pop forward and show themselves in unexpected ways. Your work will draw the viewer in, and that is a good thing.

By using tracing paper to transfer drawings from your journal to your quilt art, you can incorporate precise imagery into your work. Fluid and lyrical machine-drawn motifs, botanical illustrations, or clearly defined words with interesting fonts can help illuminate and broaden the scope of what you are trying to communicate.

To transfer a tracing-paper drawing to your quilt, you'll need:

- ◆ Design
- ◆ Projector
- ◆ Your map
- ◆ Tracing paper
- ◆ Pins
- ◆ Quilt sandwich

Note: Enlarging your imagery may be necessary.

Fig. 2A

Fig. 2B

To apply these tracings to the front of the work:

1. Resize and project your design, finding a suitable placement on your map.
2. Trace the design onto tracing paper and pin it to the front of your quilt sandwich **(Figures 1A and 1B)**.
3. Machine sew through the drawn line, tying off as you go **(Figures 2A and 2B)**.
4. Tear the paper away, pulling toward your sewn line.

This technique also works well when sewn over already quilted areas; audition your thread to make sure it is dark enough to show up (Figure 1B)!

Tip Practice Makes Perfect

With practice, you will learn control and be able to stop your machine just where you started. Practice will cure any ills here. The goal is to sew a seamless line and tie off on the back of the work so no little blubs of thread occur on the front.

Cutting Away the Organza

Cutting away the organza layer of your design, a form of reverse appliqué, can add dramatic pop and dazzle to your quilt art, revealing the broadcloth layer and colors beneath. Designs can be sewn using the tracing-paper technique prior to quilting, and then the organza can be carefully cut away within the specified area. You will need a pair of sharp and narrow embroidery scissors to pierce a small hole in the organza and then cut away the fabric. This technique is extremely gratifying and an easy way to get satisfying results.

To trim away organza layer, you'll need:

+ Tracing paper
+ Design
+ Sharp, narrow embroidery scissors
+ Quilt sandwich
+ Pins

1. Trace the design to be cut way onto tracing paper.
2. Trim close to the traced image.
3. Snip into the tracing, just up to the edge of the drawn line.
4. When you are ready to place the motif, wedge the snip around your needle, and pin the tracing paper in place.
5. Machine sew through the tracing paper.
6. Leaving the needle in the design, rip the paper away.
7. Continue quilting.
8. Once quilting is complete, pierce the organza with sharp embroidery scissors and trim cloth away, revealing the layers below.

Compare these two pieces. Pop and dazzle were added to the piece at right by cutting away the organza that covered the birds and some of the machine-drawn Xs.

Tip Cutting Organza

Cutting away the organza is exciting! Using extremely pointy, narrow-tipped embroidery scissors, slip the pointy edge into the area you wish to cut away. Cut about 1/8" (3 mm) from your sewn line. You may find that angling the top edge of your scissors toward the sewn edge will help you cut this closely.

Starry, Starry Bird, 20" × 25" (51 × 63.5 cm). Organza: Freezer-paper-resist female form, monoprint. Broadcloth: Freezer-paper-resist scroll-work, stamp, direct-dye paint. Collage, tracing-paper drawing, machine quilting, organza cut away, machine embroidery, ⅛" (3 mm) French binding.

Darkening and Accenting with Tulle

Synthetic tulle, a sheer, netted fabric, comes in a variety of colors and can be used to gently shade an area of quilting or provide a bold contrast when multiple layers are heavily quilted over. The nice thing about tulle is that it is sheer enough to darken but also allows the layers underneath to show through. If you find that your artwork is in need of a grounding type of horizon, try adding tulle while quilting.

Play with the colors you have available to you. If your piece is predominately green, for example, and needs an area of dark contrast, try layering first a single, then a double, layer of red tulle over the area in question. If that isn't quite right, move on to other colors in turn until you land the right coloring.

One of the other great things about tulle is that it is easy to cut away from your work, and you don't even need to take it out from under the needle—just pull the tulle away from your work and drag you scissors against the taut edge. Think of tulle as your quick-fix way to darken an area of your work.

To accent with tulle, you'll need:

+ Pins
+ Tulle
+ Quilt sandwich
+ Sharp, pointy embroidery scissors

1. Place and pin a layer or two of tulle over the entire area to be shaded (**Figures 1 and 2**).
2. Sew right up to but not over your major design elements.
3. Using sharp and pointy embroidery scissors, cut away unwanted tulle as close as possible.

Fig. 1

Fig. 2

Dreamy Bird, 8¾" × 7½" (22 × 19 cm). Organza: Freezer-paper-resist bird and vines, monoprint, thick-and-thin line. Broadcloth: Freezer-paper-resist bird and vines, monoprint, stamp. Machine quilting, tulle overlay, whipstitched border, fusible web with metal leaf, sequins, beads, and gold leaf.

Fig. 1

Fig. 2

Fig. 3

Quilting in Gradation

A gradation is a series of color changes within a similar palette. Machine quilting in gradation is a simple and effective way to deepen and develop the colors in your surface-designed works.

To quilt in gradation, you'll need:

- Three or four color gradations
- Quilt sandwich
- Sewing machine with free-motion capability
- Darning foot

1. Choose a gradation of three or four colors that work well with your project.
2. Starting with your darkest color, sew up to and around your major design elements **(Figure 1)**.
3. Stagger the edge where the next lighter color will be applied. This encourages the eye to travel over and not get stuck on straight lines or abrupt color changes **(Figure 2)**.
4. Tie and bury your threads.
5. Proceed systematically with your next lighter colors until satisfied **(Figure 3)**.

Tucking Silk Sheers

There may be times when a composition is lacking. Perhaps you overlooked a sparsely printed area, and your eye keeps getting stuck as it travels over the piece. Never fear! This can be remedied by tucking printed bits of silk organza between your two layers. As long as you have enough room to tuck a new motif between your two layers, you are good to go! A hemostatic clamp works well to place these small cutouts between the organza and the broadcloth, especially when space is tight.

This is when a stash of previously printed silk organza comes in handy. Or you might try printing up some black-on-white designs on organza and putting them aside just for this purpose (without washing the soda ash out); tuck the printed organza under your top layer to see whether the unprinted ground is glaring or whether it sinks well into the design. If it is glaring, a very slight application of a similar color to your artwork will knock the white back and make the additional motif fit in perfectly. However, this slows down the process some because you will need to both batch and wash the piece prior to being able to tuck it between the layers.

To tuck in silk sheers, you'll need:

- Printed motifs on organza **(Figure 1)**
- Quilt sandwich
- Hemostatic clamp

1. Trim the motif to within ⅛" (3 mm) of the printed area.
2. Insert it between the quilt layers, using the hemostatic clamp, if necessary **(Figure 2)**.
3. Quilt.

Fig. 1

Below you see some of the printed Xs at left have been cut and tucked between the layers of broadcloth and organza. They await quilting.

Fig. 2

Free-Motion Machine Quilting (aka Journal to Machine-Quilting Sampler)

I am a process person. I enjoy the act of making a thing. It does not matter how long it takes or how detailed and intricate the design; in fact, the longer it takes, the happier I am. I love the finished product and am happy to have made the art. But I much prefer the process of making the artwork to the finished object itself. I don't plot out the free-motion machine quilting, but I do assess what I would like to accentuate. I audition threads by laying a single strand over an area, and I self-search to see whether a particular motif pops into my mind for the work of art I am assessing.

Free-motion quilting is another instance where texture and differences in texture can really elevate a design; areas of calm (no stitching) alongside densely quilted areas are important. In addition to being a basic artistic concept, this creates the "puffiness" that is central to the quilt medium.

Sewing machines sew in straight lines with the assistance of the feed dogs, or the teeth found in the faceplate below the needle. You will need to drop your feed dogs, disengaging the machine from being able to sew in a straight line, and install a darning or free-motion foot. The darning foot smoothes out the area around where the needle will enter the cloth, acting as a tiny momentary hoop.

{ *Tip* **Sandwich Experiments**
Rather than try an idea out on your beautiful whole-cloth quilt design, make a small quilt sandwich and experiment on it instead. Save these trials in your three-ring binder.

Journaled drawing of daisies using a grid to play with a variety of lines and textures.

Experiment!

This is a great journal-to-machine-quilting sampler project. In your journal, lightly draw a 2" (5 cm) grid in pencil over the entire page. Choose a subject and begin to draw in pencil over the grid. Remain aware of your grid and use it to help maintain correct proportion and height of your chosen object. Draw what you see, not what you expect to see.

When the drawing is to your satisfaction, use a favorite pen to fill each section of the grid with lines and marks. Vary the distance and thickness of the lines; experiment. Draw right up to, but not over, your pencil marks. Slowly, your pencil drawing will emerge into the thick and varied lines of a drawing in pen and ink.

Proceed as if to tracing-paper machine draw: enlarge the design and trace onto tracing paper. Your quilt sandwich should be white, and your machine-drawn image and grid will also be sewn in white. Baste and sew a grid (the size of the grid should be proportioned according to the size of your drawing). Pin your tracing-paper drawing in place, drop your feed dogs, and sew through the paper according to your drawing. Rip the tracing paper away and remove any basting pins.

With contrasting thread, see how many of the hand-drawn lines you can replicate with machine quilting. Create new lines and patterns as needed. Remember to quilt up to, but not over, your white sewn line. With practice, new patterns and ideas will emerge spontaneously.

1   2   3

4   5   6   7

8   9   10

11   12   13

14   15   16

A journal
to machine-
stitch
sample.

What you see at left is my Journal to Machine Quilting Sampler explained on pages 78 and 79.

1. Feed dogs engaged, straight sewn lines, using back option to create the thick areas.
2. Feed dogs down, free-motion horizontal lines.
3. Stippling.
4. Masking-tape squares, free-motion diagonal lines.
5. Free-motion thread gradation using three shades of blue.
6. Free-motion multidirectional lines.
7. Free-motion vertical overlapping lines.
8. Masking tape ⅛" (3 mm) wide was used as a machine-quilting resist, stippling.
9. Free-motion dovetail lines.
10. Free-motion vertical lines with circles; remainder of space filled with horizontal free-motion lines. Try cutting and ironing freezer-paper circles to demarcate your own design, then sew directly to and around each circle.
11. Top right: single layer tulle; free-motion lines in both vertical and horizontal orientation, creating a grid.
12. Free-motion circles.
13. Free-motion stylized twigs; remainder of space free-motion horizontal lines.
14. Masking tape, free-motion horizontal lines.
15. Top right two layers: tulle; middle section: one layer tulle; and bottom left: no tulle; free-motion stippling in single color.
16. Free-motion vertical and intermittent horizontal straight lines with tracing-paper machine-drawn bug.

Each application discussed in this chapter—from preparing to quilt by creating machine-drawn lines to finding that a design could use the last-minute addition of some more motifs to getting down to the nitty-gritty of free-motion quilting—has added depth and perspective to your artwork. We aren't finished yet. Next up, we will address the surface of the quilt.

Remember the basics: texture and differences in texture are the keys to successful designs. Beads, sequins, embroidery, and gold leaf can be a dynamic way to push the work even further in that direction. In the next chapter, we will embrace these additional surface treatments and appeal to our inner magpie, who seeks glimmer and sparkle at every turn.

The Captain, 11" × 9" (28 × 23 cm). Organza: Freezer-paper-resist figure monoprint, thick-and thin-line. Broadcloth: Freezer-paper-resist figure, monoprint. Collage, tulle overlay, machine quilting, whipstitched binding.

Now that your quilt has been collaged and quilted, it is time to add surface embellishments. Embroidery, beads, and even gold leaf create further textural layers. Embellishment is a great way to add small bits of dazzle, brightening and highlighting areas that might otherwise recede into the background of the work. Because beading and embroidery are added to the top of the work, it lends a sense of depth, creates a shadow, and accentuates the color of your design.

Handstitched Embellishment

Hand-dyed embroidery flosses, silks, rayons, and cottons add their own flair, changing gradations of color and sheen, not to mention adding color that cannot be found anywhere else; they are your own hand-dyed threads, after all! Beading among these colorful stitches adds glamour and an almost secretive allure. Seed beads, teardrops, bugles, and charlottes become riches and gems, catching the eye with glitter and appeal. The gold leaf adds pure "bling," creating a blast of metallic shine that offsets the beads and integrates all the parts into a whole.

To add handstitched embellishments, you'll simply need crewel needles, Thread Heaven, a thimble, an office nubby, and embroidery floss. The use of an office nubby (a rubber finger-shaped filing assist) helps you pull the needle and embroidery floss through densely quilted areas with less strain on your wrists and hands. Find one that fits your index finger comfortably without pulling off your finger.

Tie this in ...
Hand-Dyeing Embroidery Floss

Hand-dyed embroidery floss is a beautiful edge addition to the surface of any quilted work of art and can also be a fantastic edge finish (see page 99). Embroidery threads come in a variety of types, from six-strand cotton, rayon, and silk, to pearl cotton, which comes in several weights. Some machine threads work well, too. And don't forget, needlepoint stores have a wide variety of threads not found in craft stores.

For the purpose of hand-dyed thread, we'll be using white thread, but many of the companies that produce embroidery threads have variegated threads that are well worth checking out.

Hand-dyed threads just have a luster and vibrancy that cannot be beat! Follow these easy steps to dye your own embroidery floss.

To hand-dye floss, you'll need:
- A variety of embroidery flosses
- DMC StitchBow floss holders
- Soda ash (see page 19)
- Bucket
- Ziplock plastic sandwich bags
- 3 syringes
- Dye concentrates in red, blue, and yellow

1. Place or wind the floss onto the floss holder.
2. Soak floss on holder in soda ash for 30 minutes.
3. Place floss (holder and all) in plastic sandwich bag. The floss should be wet but not sitting in a puddle of soda ash.
4. Use a syringe for each of three dye concentrates: red, blue, and yellow.
5. For variegated threads, mix two colors. You'll need no more than 1 teaspoon of dye per color. A little bit of color goes a long way. You may want to mix urea water into the dye to lessen the intensity of the color.
6. Apply the lighter color first to just one side of the floss, seal the bag, and gently massage the floss.
7. Apply the darker color to the opposite side of the floss and massage gently. Allow to sit for 1 to 4 hours.
8. Rinsing the dye out is a gentle affair; you do not want the threads to become agitated and knot up. Fill a bucket with water and allow the water to settle. Gently place the floss in the water and leave to soak. Remove the floss, change the water, and gently place the floss back in the water. You may need to do this several times, until the water runs clear.
9. Allow to dry on the floss holder. Once dry, the floss is ready to use!

EMBROIDERY

When I use embroidery, I assess the piece just after I have done the machine quilting. It is possible to push the piece further, darkening an area with a thick application of embroidery, making a light area pop by adding even lighter dashes of embroidery, or interspersing the embroidery with beads or perhaps even some gold leaf.

Think of embroidery as a tool. It can help ground a work, accentuate an important area, or add either a gentle bit of texture or a profusion of it; there are no limitations, except time and patience. Embroidery adds another element of texture and difference in texture, which can be considered a type of artistic tension.

Perhaps you have a piece with a gentle application of dye and you feel that adding tiny embroidered ditties, Vs, dashes, or French knots of a lightly colored single strand of floss will accentuate and bring your printing to the forefront. Or perhaps a really heavy application of six-strand floss will round the piece out, creating a quality of earthiness. Embroidery is the solution! Almost every mark you can create on paper is fair game with needle and thread.

There is a wealth of flosses on the market. Silk pulls through the work like butter and shines with a luster that cannot be found elsewhere. Rayon is incredibly lustrous, and cottons are beautiful, too! Each holds and reflects dye wonderfully and can be dyed to match your project precisely or to contrast purposefully.

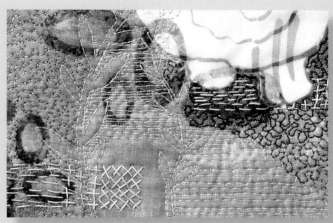

Fig. 1

CROSS-STITCH

Cross-stitch can be sewn in columns, blocks, or horizontal lines. When working with cross-stitch, use a steady hand and do your best to create the Xs in a similar shape and size (**Figure 1**). Once you have a grid or row established, this becomes much easier.

When handstitching, use supportive techniques, such as masking tape, to help define an area. Masking tape can remind you not to sew past the taped edge, and it can create a horizon line (**Figure 2**). Freezer paper can be cut into shapes and ironed in place. These reminders mark out an area, making it easier for you to produce crisp lines and motifs. Leaving some areas without any embellishment is critical; texture and differences in texture are an important artistic concept to embrace.

Fig. 2

That's Monk!, 11" × 10" (28 × 25 cm). Organza: Freezer-paper resist, monoprint, thick-and-thin line. Broadcloth: Freezer-paper resist, freezer-paper screen-print stencil, collage, machine quilting, hand embroidery.

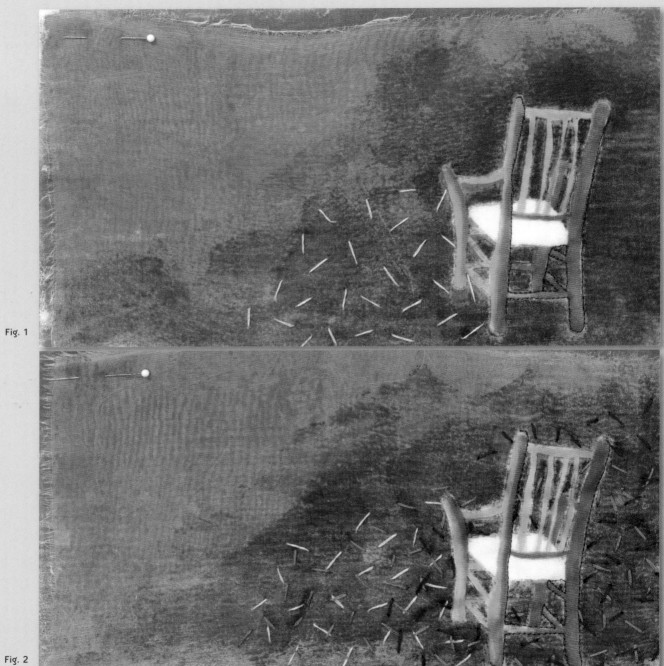

Fig. 1

Fig. 2

Fig. 3. The finished piece.

CHICKEN SCRATCH

Chicken scratch is a scattering of short, evenly spaced, randomly angled stitches that can be used to accent or define an area of your quilt. You might use a single layer and color of embroidery floss, or you might layer an overlapping gradation of color from light to dark to make a highly textural motif.

To embellish with chicken scratch:

1. Start with the lightest color first, in the farthest placement from the motif you will accentuate. Work toward your main motif **(Figure 1)**.
2. With the second color of the gradation, begin to overlap some but not all of the lightest color. Work toward the main motif **(Figure 2)**.
3. Work in this manner until you are satisfied with the results **(Figure 3)**.

DASHES, DOTS, AND BUSY BITS OF NOISE
Try working with embroidery in an intuitive manner. If it feels right, commit the stitch to cloth and don't think about the effect. Continue until your inner voice tells you to stop.

In creating *Flicker* (page 89), I made my machine quilting mimic the texture of the monoprinted dark background and flow upward in the same direction the bird is flying. In assessing the piece, I decided the handstitching should do the same and also wanted to ground the piece from the lower left upward in a gradation by using a heavy application of varying thicknesses of floss. Aesthetically, I made the decision that beads and sequins should hug the bird's head and appear nowhere else.

I wanted this embroidery application to be even darker than my printed ground, so I used black, blue, and sometimes plum cotton embroidery floss to achieve this. Chicken scratch, Xs, Vs—everything was fair game in the creation of this piece. Intuitively, I added tiny rows of what I call bars; I took up two threads' worth of cloth with my embroidery needle and sewed repetitively in straight lines. This created a ridge, or bar, of embroidery stitches. I do not know whether this stitch has a name, but it occurred to me because the piece needed some sparkle. This

was an intuitive approach, and one I hope you will embrace, too.

On a simpler note, perhaps your work will need just a slight touch, a scattering of stitches that serve to imitate tiny springs of grass with a few sequins dotting the ground, as with *Little Wren*. The aesthetic of the piece will dictate the intensity of the surface treatment.

Just have fun with it, let go, and see what happens. Approach embroidery as a way to make marks, lines, and areas of extreme texture or shading. With all the luster of your own hand-dyed threads, jump in with both feet and embrace this additional surface treatment. Make your art sing and push it beyond any preconceived ideas you might have had about embroidery.

Little Wren, 4½" × 7¼" (11.5 × 18.5 cm). Machine-drawn line, tulle, machine quilting, embroidery, beading, whipstitched binding.

Below: *Blueberry Deer*, 4" × 6" (10 × 15 cm). Broadcloth, tulle, machine-drawn line, machine quilting, embroidery, whipstitched binding.

Above: *Flicker*, 6½" × 9½" (16.5 × 24 cm). Broadcloth monoprinting, freezer-paper resists, machine quilting, beading, embroidery, and whipstitched binding using both commercial and hand-dyed threads.

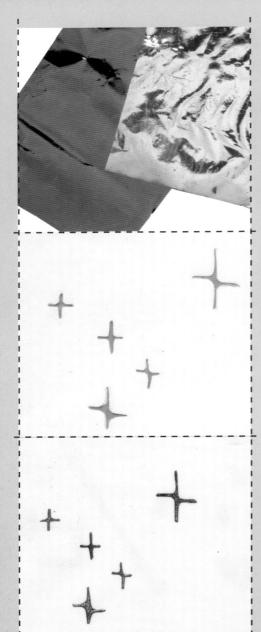

The above sample was done on muslin specifically for reference in a three-ring binder.

Gold Foil and Gold Leaf Embellishment

If handstitching is not how you see your quilt being embellished, you can use gold foil and gold leaf, applying them to your quilt with adhesive or fusible web. There are several ways to do this. You might choose to use a freezer-paper stencil with specific glues, to pulverize fusible web in a coffee grinder, or to apply a precut square of fusible web directly to metal leaf. Each technique has its own special needs. Once applied, always use an ironing cloth to protect the foil or metal leaf from tarnishing.

I suggest you do samples, created exclusively for your binder, to teach yourself how to use freezer-paper stencils with glue and gold foil, pulverized fusible web with gold foil, and fusible web applied directly to gold leaf. Play with the techniques. See what comes of it, then save the samples in your binder.

To make sample pages for your three-ring binder, you'll need:

- Cloth
- Masking tape
- Iron
- Hole puncher

1. Cut a 16" × 11" (41 × 28 cm) piece of cloth.
2. Tape the shorter two edges with masking tape to strengthen them.
3. Iron in half widthwise.
4. Punch holes with an office supply hole puncher through taped edges.

FREEZER-PAPER STENCIL WITH GLUE AND GOLD FOIL

It is somewhat counterintuitive to apply gold leaf after machine quilting, but why not? Using a freezer-paper stencil to apply glue to a previously quilted area adds even more texture! The glue will adhere to the machine-sewn stitches differently than to the plain areas of cloth. It can't be beat.

It is always a good idea to create a test quilting sample, to iron out the kinks of the technique and to perfect your application of glue.

Remember, metallic foil has a shiny side and a dull side. The dull side gets adhered to the glue; once peeled away, the metallic shiny layer remains on your quilt surface.

To create a freezer-paper stencil to apply gold leaf, you'll need:

- Iron
- Freezer-paper stencil
- Quilt sandwich
- Squeegee
- Screen-Trans Foil-On Textile Transfer Adhesive
- Gold foil (I used Jones Tones here)

For this application, you will create a freezer-paper stencil as described in Chapter 1 (see page 28).

Rococo Bluebird, 10¼" × 9" (26 × 23 cm). Organza: Freezer-paper-resist scrollwork and bird, monoprint. Broadcloth: Freezer-paper-resist bird, monoprint, stamp, direct-dye paint. Collage (brown scrollwork), machine quilting, freezer-paper-stencil gold leaf, cut away organza over bird, whipstitched binding.

To apply freezer-paper-stencil gold leaf:

1. Iron the stencil in place on your quilt. The quilt stitches may inhibit the freezer paper from fully adhering; check carefully and iron with a firm hand. Check again.
2. Gently squeegee the adhesive onto the quilt through the stencil. You want a thick buildup of adhesive.
3. Allow to fully dry.
4. Remove the freezer paper.
5. Place the foil, dull side down, on top of the applied adhesive.
6. Using the edge of a heated iron as if it were a burnishing tool, iron the foil to the adhesive.
7. Allow to cool completely.
8. Peel away the foil.

Pulverized Fusible Web

PULVERIZED FUSIBLE WEB WITH GOLD FOIL

Pulverizing fusible web creates a powder that can be sprinkled on to create an organic smattering of sparkle and glitz. It takes just a few minutes to do, can be stored indefinitely in a baggie, and gives successful results with little effort.

To pulverize fusible web, you'll need:

- Fusible web
- Coffee grinder
- Re-sealable jar
- Quilt sandwich
- Gold foil
- Iron

1. Peel the fusible web from the protective backing.
2. Tear the fusible web into palm-size pieces and fill the grinder.
3. Grind to a fine powder.
4. Place the pulverized fusible web in the re-sealable jar and continue grinding the remaining pieces until all the intended fusible web is pulverized.
5. Scatter the pulverized web over your quilt.
6. Place the foil, dull side down, on your quilt.
7. Using the edge of a heated iron as if it were a burnishing tool, iron the foil to the pulverized fusible web.
8. Allow to cool completely.
9. Peel the foil away.

Gold foil applied to muslin by ironing. These three samples were created on muslin for my three-ring binder.

Gold leaf foil slightly peeled away.

The completed binder sample, gold foil removed.

Odd Chair, 8" × 10¼" (20 × 26 cm). Organza: Freezer-paper-resist chair, monoprinted, thick-and-thin line. Broadcloth: Soy-wax circle, stamped, monoprinted. Organza cut away to expose cotton, machine quilting, pulverized fusible with gold foil, whipstitched border.

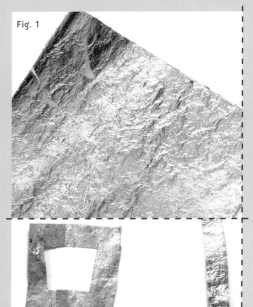
Fig. 1

Fig. 2

FUSIBLE WEB APPLIED TO GOLD LEAF

Applying fusible web directly to gold leaf allows you to tear or cut small pieces away to be applied in spot treatment, a form of control that can be quite useful. Gold leaf is sold in books and is so light and airy that it can float away at the slightest breeze. Keep the book closed and in a safe place until needed. It's important to use an ironing sheet to prevent the leaf from tarnishing with the application of heat.

To apply fusible web to gold leaf, you'll need:

- Scissors
- Fusible web
- Gold leaf
- Ironing sheet
- Iron
- Quilt sandwich

1. Cut the fusible web ⅛" (3 mm) short of the gold leaf on all four sides.
2. Open the gold leaf booklet, leaving the gold leaf on the page.
3. Place the fusible web, glue side down, on the gold leaf.
4. Place an ironing sheet on top.
5. Iron, pressing hard; do not swish back and forth.
6. Allow to cool.
7. Remove from the gold leaf book **(Figure 1)**.
8. Tear or cut into small pieces; the glue side will appear dull **(Figure 2)**.
9. Iron the gold leaf to your quilt using an ironing sheet.

Dreamy Bird, 8¾" × 7½" (22 × 19 cm). Organza: Freezer-paper-resist bird and vines, monoprint, thick-and-thin line. Broadcloth: Freezer-paper-resist bird and vines, monoprint, stamp. Machine quilting, tulle overlay, whipstitched border, fusible web applied to metal leaf, sequins, and beads.

Beaded Embellishment

Beads are a versatile and energetic embellishment. The variation in size, shape, texture, and finish is enticing enough to break the bank! Applying beads to finish a piece of quilt art is an easy process, involving only a few materials (beads, thread, and needle).

Seed beads come in a variety of sizes. The sizing system works in an inverse manner: the larger the number, the smaller the bead. Size 13/0 beads are tiny compared to size 6/0 beads. The name seed bead is a generalized term that describes any small bead, including bugle beads, charlotte beads (a single flat cutout on a round bead that creates sparkle), and bugle beads. The finishes that beads come in includes aurora borealis (an iridescent effect), matte, and silver-lined. Whatever type, color, or finish you desire, there is a bead for every project.

Silamide is a twisted two-ply synthetic thread that is both strong and pretty and comes in a variety of colors. It is quite unlikely that this thread will break, but, as a rule, I suggest you tie off your thread every six beads or so. If your piece is functional and will receive wear and tear, tie off every third bead. This way, if one bead falls off, it will not have a domino effect on the remaining beads.

Needles are subjective. You may prefer the traditional long, thin, bendable needle found in quality beading stores. I prefer a #12 sharp. This size needle fits up to size 13/0 beads and is sturdy, rarely breaking or bending during heavy use.

BEADS

You will apply beads using a running stitch (see Glossary, page 132), which can be hidden in the layers of your quilt sandwich. Applying beads to heavily machine-quilted areas can be challenging. Remember that the front, or face, of the work is more important than the back! Wearing an office nubby on your index finger and a thimble on your middle finger will reduce strain in your fingers.

To apply beads, you'll need:

- Silamide thread
- Beading needle
- Quilt sandwich
- Small embroidery scissors
- Beads

1. Cut an 18" (46 cm) strand of Silamide and make a knot at one end. Thread your needle.
2. Bring the needle in through the back of the work, tug to hide the knot, and trim the tail, if needed.
3. Thread one bead onto the needle and bring the needle back through the same hole it came out. This is called under-cutting the bead and it helps to hide the thread under the bead **(Figure 1)**.
Bring the needle back up to the front of the work. Repeat Step 3 until you're satisfied with the result, tying off as necessary.

SEQUINS AND BEADS

You may wish to pile descending sizes of flat sequins one atop another. This works especially well with different colors of sequins. Or you might want just a single sequin attached with a bead.

To apply sequins and beads, you'll need:

- Silamide thread
- Beading needle
- Quilt sandwich
- Small embroidery scissors
- Sequins
- Beads

1. Cut an 18" (46 cm) strand of Silamide and make a knot at one end. Thread your needle.
2. Bring the needle in through the back of the work, tug to hide the knot, and trim the tail, if needed.
3. Place a sequin, then a bead onto the strand.
4. Place the needle into the sequin's eye and then back into the same hole from which the thread emerged **(Figure 2)**.
5. Bring the needle back up to the front of the work. Repeat Steps 3 and 4 until you're satisfied with the result, tying off as necessary.

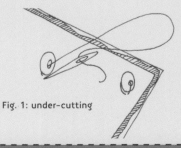

Fig. 1: under-cutting

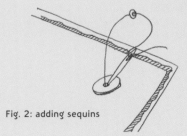

Fig. 2: adding sequins

BUGLE BEADS

Bugle beads are great fun to use as an embellishment. They are long, thin tubes with sharp edges. To be safe, you may want to thread and sew them onto the work twice. Undercut them slightly (see Step 3 under Sequins and Beads) as you attach them. You might also choose to embroider over them. One or two whipstitches are a beautiful addition to this bead embellishment (**Figure 3**).

Now that your embellishment is complete, the next step is finishing.

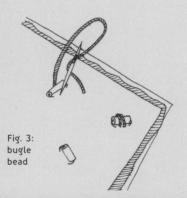

Fig. 3:
bugle
bead

Dancing Chair, 8" × 9½" (20.5 × 24 cm) (*Precarious Chair* series). Organza: Freezer-paper-resist chair, monoprint, thick-and-thin line. Broadcloth: soy wax, monoprint, stamp. Machine quilting, tracing-paper drawing, beaded, whipstitched binding, sequins, and beads.

Still Life in Time,
19¼" × 18" (49 ×
46 cm). Organza:
Freezer-paper-resist
flowers and bowls,
monoprint, thick-and
thin-lines. Broadcloth:
Freezer-paper-resist
flowers and bowls,
freezer-paper stencil
with dye crayon,
freezer-paper-stencil
screen print. Collage,
machine-quilted.

Finishing, binding, and hanging a work of art is a wonder to behold.
Deciding how to finish a piece is dependent on a few factors. Borders
hearken back to the traditional roots of quilting. For this reason, I tend to
steer clear of borders, preferring the fine-art tendency to create works of art
that extend the entire width of the "canvas" or painted surface. My bindings,
therefore, fade into the piece as a whole and are narrow and unobtrusive.
I prefer to create a monoprinted gradation that captures the two most
prominent colors in the quilt top.

Types of Finishing

I will discuss attaching the hanging sleeve and three different types of bindings, depending on the size of the work: whipstitched, French, and knife-edge bindings.

Whipstitched bindings are used for pieces smaller than 12" (30.5 cm) square. A whipstitched binding is quite a beautiful and intense finish that takes time to complete, so it is a great finish for small works. Using your own hand-dyed floss to whipstitch the binding is almost too good to be true, like dipping strawberries in chocolate. Your threads will be vibrantly colored to suit your work, have luster and sheen, and can either be roughly sewn or sewn in such a way as to show off the hand-dyed gradation.

French bindings are most often used for larger works and easily accomodate hanging sleeves.

A knife-edge binding is a good way to complete small to midsize work. The added benefit of this technique is that when you are finished quilting, your edges need no further attention, because the batting and backing have already been concealed!

Hanging Sleeve

No matter which type of binding you choose, if your intention is to hang a piece directly on the wall, you will need a hanging sleeve, and this is made before binding the quilt. The sleeve needs to be a finished 4" (10 cm) wide tube that will hold a hanging rod. Preferred hanging rods are made of aluminum, are sold in several lengths, are ⅛" (3 mm) thick, and can be purchased from your local hardware store.

The sleeve is created with a bit of ease to accommodate the width of the rod and is generally 3" (8 cm) shorter than the finished width of the work, leaving 1½" (4 cm) on either side of the finished sleeve.

Here's how to calculate the length of the sleeve.

1. Measure the width of the work.
2. Subtract 3" (8 cm).
3. Add 2" (5 cm) to clean-finish both ends. Fold the raw edge under ½" (1.3 cm), then fold again, and sew to conceal. You will have 1" (2.5 cm) on both sides of your sleeve to clean-finish, and your sleeve will be 3" (8 cm) shorter than the width of your quilt when complete.

Now you are ready to apply the sleeve:

1. Cut the appropriate size sleeve.
2. Hem the edges to clean-finish.
   a. Fold in ½" (1.3 cm).
   b. Fold in ½" (1.3 cm) again (the raw edge will be completely hidden).
   c. Sew along the folded edge.
3. With the wrong sides together, fold the sleeve in half lengthwise.

Sleeve attached.

4. The two top edges should meet ⅛" (3 mm) short of one another.
5. Iron. You have created a hard edge that will later be used as a guide to handstitch the bottom edge in place.
6. The edge that is ⅛" (3 mm) shorter will face the back of the work.
7. Bring the two raw edges together, center, and pin to the back of the work.
8. Proceed with your border and binding technique.

THE FINISH LINE

Wherever possible, try to create your own binding materials that match the main color of your artwork. Work a monoprinted gradation if your piece is large or dye your own embroidery floss if the piece is of a manageable size to whipstitch the binding. Your finishing technique should be just as beautiful as the work you have created. You will want every aspect of your finished work to sing of your great accomplishment and your attention to detail.

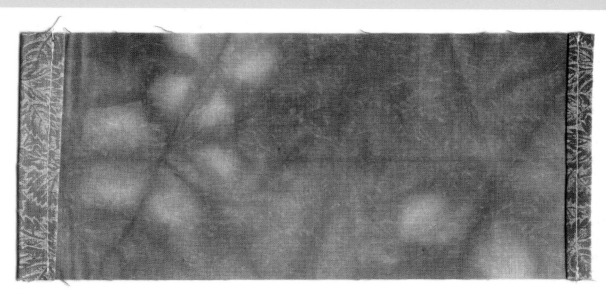

Sleeve before closed. Note hemmed edges.

Sleeve folded just short of equal.

Tip **Try a Shadow Box!**

More often than not, if a piece is small, I suggest framing the piece in a shadow-box–style frame. This type of frame has depth, and your work can be mounted in such a way that it will not touch the glass. It also gives small works a feeling of substance and respectability (see Resources, page 134).

WHIPSTITCHED BINDING

Preparing the edges of small works in preparation for a whipstitched binding helps contain loose threads and batting, and inserting gimp into the edging helps create a sturdy, substantial finish. Gimp is a coarse, thick thread that sometimes has a piece of wire in its core. Almost anything can be used as gimp—string or yarn—as long as it has body and will hold the edge of the quilt firmly in place.

To create very square corners, you will want to sew off the edge of the work. Turn 90°, creating a small thread loop on each of the four corners. For best results, use this technique for both a straight stitch and a zigzag stitch.

Bluebird, 11" × 10" (28 × 25.5 cm).

To prepare the edge, you'll need:

* Sewing machine
* Gimp or heavy cotton thread or yarn
* Scissors

1. Straight stitch a ⅛" (3 mm) seam allowance on all four sides **(Figure 1)**.
2. Satin-stitch over the gimp, concealing both the gimp and the straight-stitched line at a 2½-stitch width **(Figure 2)**.
3. Trim the gimp.

4. Do an additional satin stitch at a 3½-stitch width.

Now you are ready to whipstitch the binding:

1. Working from the front of the work, thread the strand from front to back. The knot will be at the front of the work.
2. Hold the knot and tail aside and whipstitch to conceal.

3. An occasional length of buttonhole stitch is an appealing addition.
4. There is no need to knot off when you come to the end of the strand. Turn the work to the wrong side, bury at least a 2" (5 cm) strand in the previous stitches, and then trim.
5. Continue to whipstitch around all four sides until finished.

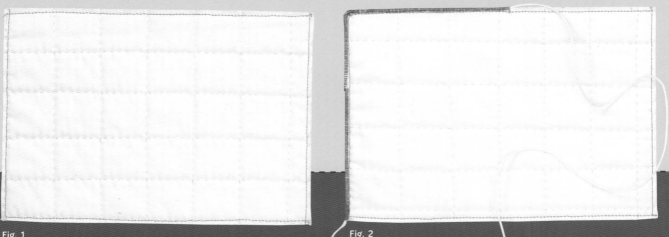

Fig. 1

Fig. 2

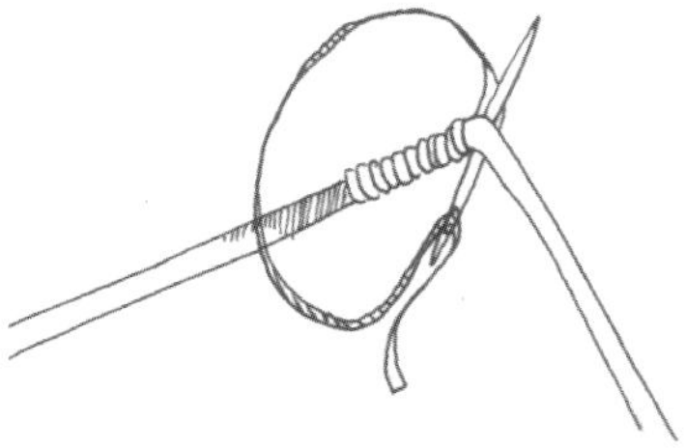

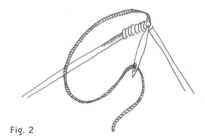

Fig. 1

Fig. 2

Tie this in ...
Mitered Corners

Embroidered mitered corners are a fantastic bit of hand-stitched magic. Whipstitch just up to the corner and then pierce the inner edge, dividing the embroidery thread in half **(Figure 1)**.

Pull the thread through the work—half the thread should turn the corner, and the other half stays on the side you just whipstitched **(Figure 2)**.

Pierce the work again, just short of the last stitch, and continue until the corner has been completely finished.

From left to right, these fabrics were created as bindings for *Fiore* (page 65), *Still Life in Time* (page 98), and *Guardians of Being* (page 59).

FRENCH BINDING

Choose two of the predominant colors within the work and create color-gradated monoprinted yardage, batch (see page 19), and wash.

To create a French binding, you'll need:

+ Ruler
+ Monoprinted gradation fabrics to match your quilt art
+ Rotary cutter
+ Self-healing mat
+ Sewing machine
+ Iron and ironing board
+ Scissors
+ Handsewing needle and thread
+ Prepared hanging sleeve (see page 100)

1. Measure all four sides of your quilt to determine how many strips of fabric you will need and cut strips of fabric 1⅛" (3 cm) wide using a rotary cutter and self-healing mat.
2. Sew the strips together, matching colors, then iron the seams open.
3. Iron the strip in half lengthwise.
4. Leaving a 5" (13 cm) tail, and beginning in the middle of one side, sew the raw edge of the binding to the front of your work, ⅛" (3 mm) from the edge.
5. Stop ⅛" (3 mm) from the next edge; turn 90° **(Figure 1)**.
6. Back up to the very edge of the work.
7. Fold the binding up and away from your machine's needle.
8. Continue sewing ⅛" (3 mm) from the raw edge.
9. When you come within 5" (13 cm) of the starting point, stop and reverse stitch or back-tack (two stitch lengths will do) to secure.
10. Butt two ends together, pinch a crease as a reminder of where they should meet and trim to accomodate a ½" (1.3 cm) seam allowance **(Figure 2)**.
11. Iron the seam allowance to the inside of the binding and sew the bindings together using this as a guide.
12. Iron open.
13. Sew down the remaining binding.
14. Snip the corners to release the turn tension.
15. Handsew the finished edge to the back of the work **(Figure 3)**.
16. Sew hanging sleeve in place **(Figure 4)**.

Fig. 1

Fig. 2

Fig. 3

Fig. 4

Fig. 1

Fig. 2

KNIFE-EDGE BINDING

Sometimes a hard-edged finish is just what is needed. This binding truly extends all the way to the finished edge of the work—no French binding or whipstitched edge here. The quilt art extends all the way to the edge and over to the back of the work. The front of the quilt art will be folded over the batting, which will be cut to the finished size of the work. This technique works best on midsize to small works. Try as you might, it is quite difficult to keep the artwork perfectly square. Still, this is a beautiful way to finish a work.

If you decide on a knife-edge binding, you will prepare the work for this finish *prior* to quilting it.

To create a knife-edge binding, you'll need:

* Ruler
* Quilt top
* Rotary cutter
* Batting
* Iron and ironing board
* Basting thread
* Backing
* Glue stick

1. Measure the quilt top.
2. Cut the batting at least ½" (1.3 cm) shorter than the quilt top on all four sides.
3. Place the quilt top and batting facedown on your ironing surface.
4. Working on two opposite sides, fold the overlapping edges up and over the batting and iron in place.
5. Working on the other two opposite sides, fold the overlapping edges up and over the batting and iron in place. Undercut the corners so you cannot see the folded edge from the front.
6. Baste **(Figure 1)**.
7. Cut a backing piece ¼" (6 mm) larger than the quilt top on all four sides.
8. Using a glue stick, dab each of the four corners and turn as if to create a ⅜" (1 cm) dog-ear **(Figure 2)**.
9. Run a length of glue on each of the four edges and turn under ⅜" (1 cm). You have now made the backing slightly smaller than the artwork.
10. Sew backing in place **(Figure 3)**.
11. Quilt **(Figure 4)**.

Now we can say that we are truly finished!

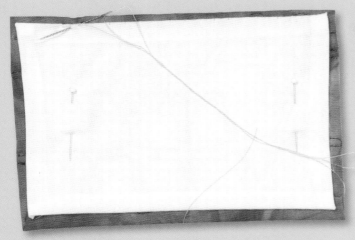

Fig. 3

Fig. 4

Self Portrait (ATC),
2½" × 3½" (6.5
× 9 cm). Organza:
Freezer-paper-resist
figure, monoprint,
thick-and-thin line.
Broadcloth: mono-
print, stamp. Knife-
edge finish, machine
quilting.

After creating larger works of art you might find that you are creatively spent. This time becomes important as a means to reconnect with yourself and provides an opportunity to assess growth and direction. It also allows you to move out of your studio with all its dyes, brushes, soy wax, and textile-related media and into the pages of your journal. Give yourself the freedom to explore and experiment on a smaller scale. Sometimes you will create little pieces of shining brilliance—or you might want to hide the piece at the bottom of a very full trash can—but because you are working in a small format, these explorations are easy to do.

Super collectible ATCs (artist trading cards) made in groups to create a single image are highly sought after! Gouache, stamping, and collage on playing cards.

Working Small

Working small also enables you to draw out and aerate your creative center, permitting the release of the last work you were so deeply entrenched in, liberating you with playful abandon.

Working in a small format allows you to flesh out an idea and its execution for larger works without using major amounts of cloth or art supplies. Not that all small pieces necessarily lead to larger works, but there is a fine tradition of working in miniature that should not be ignored. Small works ask the viewer to lean in, to think about and become momentarily entranced.

They are little bits of sweet beauty.

Working small is also a way to investigate a single design motif repetitively in a series. Working in series is an important concept for every artist. It provides an opportunity to build a cohesive body of work in a discernable style. There is an endless sense of possibility in playing with the same form over multiple pieces of art and some comfort, too, in knowing that you need not reinvent the creative wheel with each and every piece.

For instance, chairs cannot truly be separated from their use in supporting the human form. There is a solitude and grace in viewing a chair. You might wonder about what activities a chair has endured: dinners eaten, books read, or a grandchild held in sleepy stupor. Or you might see a dilapidated chair on top of a trash heap in an overgrown alley.

You can depict your chosen subject in exact detail or rummage around your imagination, as I did when creating the *Precarious Chairs* series, which includes three-legged and off-kilter chairs (see pages 120–127).

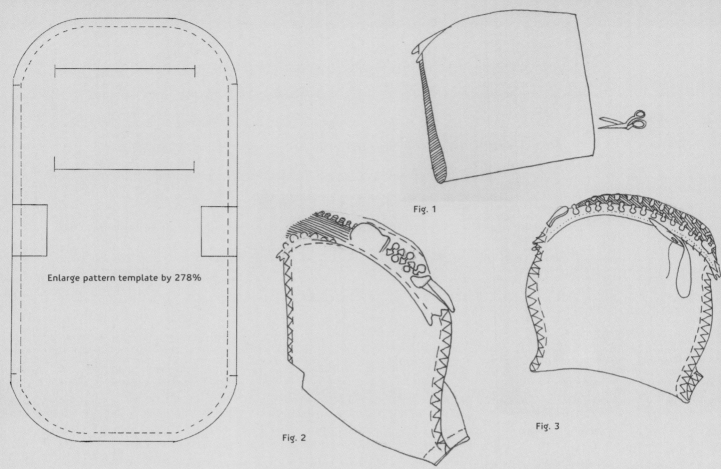

Enlarge pattern template by 278%

Fig. 1

Fig. 2

Fig. 3

Pretty Purse Pattern

This small project can be whipped up for a quick gift.

You'll need:

* Fabric
* Batting
* Backing fabric
* Sewing machine
* Scissors
* Pattern (see above), enlarged 278%
* Zipper (see Resources, page 134)
* Handsewing needle and thread

1. Create fabric for the face of the purse using 1" (2.5 cm) more fabric on all four sides than the pattern calls for.
2. Sandwich the face, batting, and backing, then quilt the three layers together.
3. Cut out the basic pattern. Do not cut the notches in the middle of the pattern because these will be cut later.
4. Set the zipper **(Figure 1)**.
5. Trim the face, batting, and backing below the zipper tape to half of the original seam allowance.
6. Open the zipper halfway.

7. Sew a ¼" (6 mm) seam allowance in straight stitch down each side of the purse. Zigzag the raw edges to finish.
8. Cut the notch on each side of the bottom edge.
9. Pinch the cutouts open. Sew a ¼" (6 mm) seam allowance. Zigzag the raw edge to finish **(Figure 2)**. Handsew the zipper tape to conceal the raw edges of the quilt sandwich **(Figure 3)**.
10. Turn right side out.

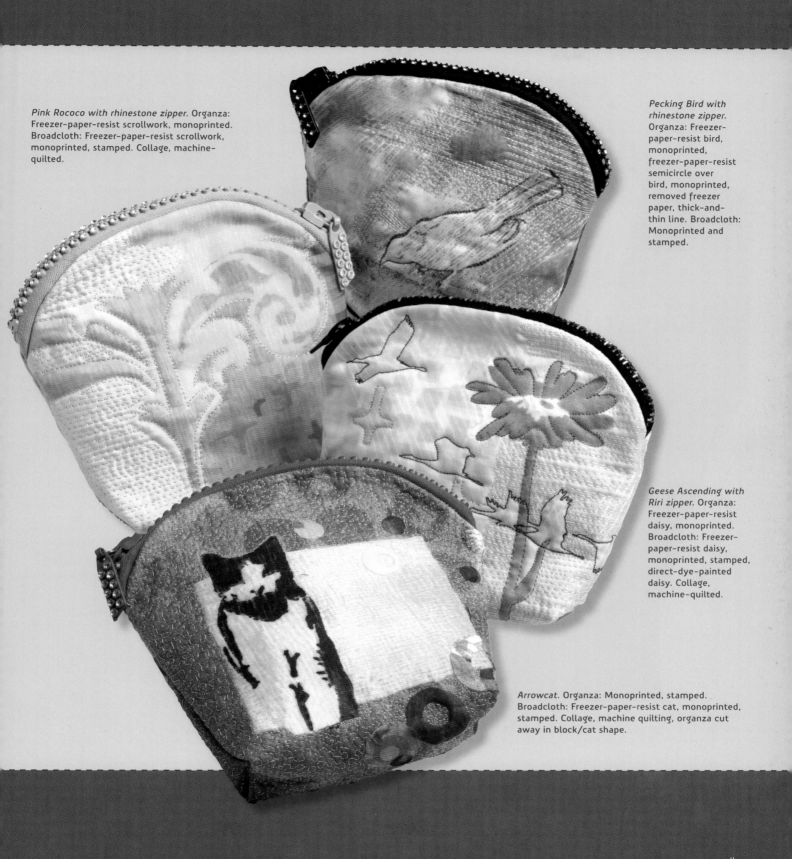

Pink Rococo with rhinestone zipper. Organza: Freezer-paper-resist scrollwork, monoprinted. Broadcloth: Freezer-paper-resist scrollwork, monoprinted, stamped. Collage, machine-quilted.

Pecking Bird with rhinestone zipper. Organza: Freezer-paper-resist bird, monoprinted, freezer-paper-resist semicircle over bird, monoprinted, removed freezer paper, thick-and-thin line. Broadcloth: Monoprinted and stamped.

Geese Ascending with Riri zipper. Organza: Freezer-paper-resist daisy, monoprinted. Broadcloth: Freezer-paper-resist daisy, monoprinted, stamped, direct-dye-painted daisy. Collage, machine-quilted.

Arrowcat. Organza: Monoprinted, stamped. Broadcloth: Freezer-paper-resist cat, monoprinted, stamped. Collage, machine quilting, organza cut away in block/cat shape.

Sewing Holster. Organza: Freezer-paper-resist Chinese character, monoprint, freezer-paper-stencil Os, monoprint, thick-and-thin line. Broadcloth: soy wax, direct-dye paint, stamp, ghost print of Os. Collage, machine-quilted.

Sewing Holster

Make a sewing holster for a friend to hold all of her sewing supplies. Handmade gifts given to our fellow quilt artists and sewing fashionistas are always the most well-received gifts imaginable!

HARD-PAPER PATTERN

Creating a hard-paper pattern will allow you to use and reuse this pattern freely. The hard edge of the pattern allows you to use a pen to trace the pattern onto your intended fabric prior to cutting it out; cutting just inside this mark will eliminate it. In my opinion, this is a much better alternative to the tissue paper patterns we generally use.

To create a hard-paper pattern, you'll need:

- 40" (102 cm) of craft paper or brown paper grocery bag
- Pattern (see page 115), enlarged 250%
- Stapler
- Paper scissors

1. Fold the craft paper in half widthwise.
2. Butt the enlarged pattern pieces up to the folded edge of the craft paper when suggested. Staple in place.
3. Cut out the pattern and remove the staples. The pattern can now be opened as needed.

CREATE THE HOLSTER

You will be making blanks. Baste a quilt sandwich larger than the pattern piece calls for, machine quilt, *then* place the pattern piece atop the blank and cut the intended shape. Each pattern piece—the neck piece, the pockets, and the pin book flap—will need its own blank.

To make the holster, you'll need:

◆ Fabrics
◆ Batting
◆ Small piece of felt
◆ Sewing machine
◆ Scissors
◆ Pins
◆ Small magnet (placed inside the pin book, this will allow you to quickly hold pins and needles! A nifty addition; see page 114).

From Fabric

1. Cut two 5" × 42" (13 × 107 cm) pieces of cloth for the Sewing Holster blank— one art quilt, one backing.
2. Cut two 5" × 8" (13 × 20 cm) pieces of cloth for pocket blanks.
3. Cut one 5" × 7" (13 × 18 cm) piece of cloth for pin book flap.
4. Cut three 1⅛" (4 cm) wide strips for French binding technique (see page 104).

From Batting

1. Cut one 5" × 42" (13 × 107 cm) piece of batting for Holster.
2. Cut two 5" × 4" (13 × 10 cm) pieces of batting for Pockets.
3. Using pattern piece, cut one batting for Pin Book Flap.

From Felt

1. Using pattern piece, cut one felt piece for Pin Book.
2. Using the two 5" × 42" (13 × 107 cm) fabric strips, create a quilt sandwich with the batting.
3. Quilt.
4. Pin the Holster pattern atop this blank and cut.
5. Put aside.

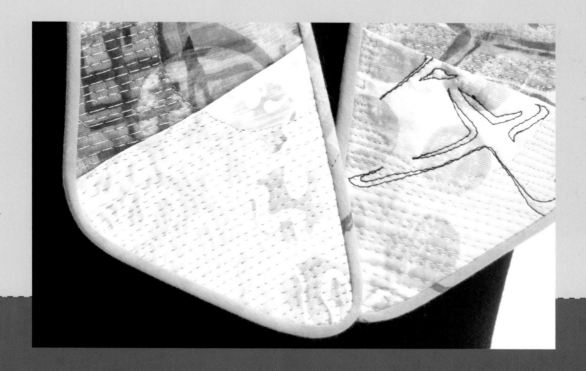

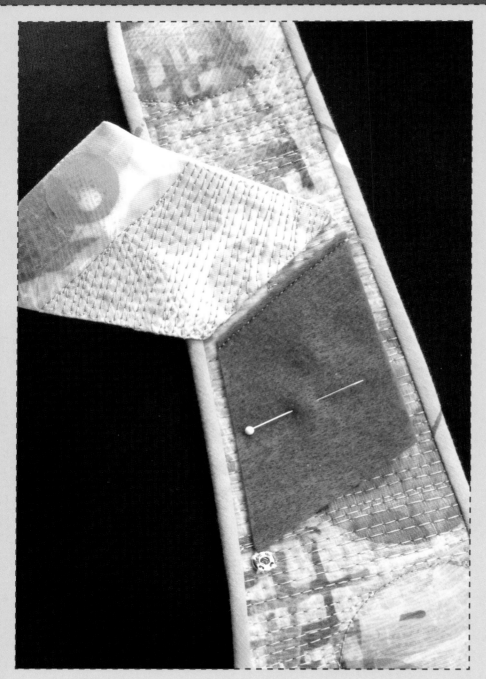

A small magnet placed inside the pin book holds pins and needles.

Create the Pockets

Fold the 5" × 8" (13 × 20 cm) fabric over each piece of 5" × 4" (13 × 10 cm) batting. The folded edge becomes the finished top edge of the pocket (**Figure 1**).

1. Quilt.
2. Place the quilted pockets, right sides together, with the top edges aligned with one another. Pin the Pocket pattern in place and cut.
3. Put aside.

MAKE THE PIN BOOK

1. Place open Pin Book pattern piece on top of the 5" × 7" (13 × 18 cm) piece of cloth.
2. Pin and cut.
3. Fold in half, right sides together.
4. Place the batting for the Pin Book on the folded fabric, butting it up to the folded edge and centering it (**Figure 2**). This piece of batting is cut so that a ¼" (6 mm) seam will overlap the batting by just a tad, *just* catching the batting in the seam.

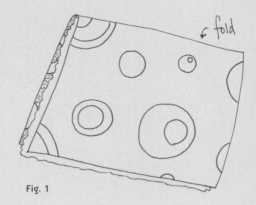

Fig. 1

5. Sew along the three edges, leave an opening to turn.
6. Turn.
7. Tuck the raw open edge under.
8. Tuck a magnet into the Pin Book, with the right side facing toward the front, not the batting.
9. Handsew the opening shut.
10. Quilt up to and around the magnet.

ASSEMBLE

1. Place the pockets, aligning the curved cut edge of the pocket with the curved cut edge of the holster, and pin in place.
2. Following the directions for the French binding (page 104), machine sew the binding in place, securing the pockets as you do so.
3. Place the pin book felt according to the pattern, pin, and machine sew in place.
4. Pin the Pin Book Flap piece over the top and handsew.

Note: You may want to sew a snap in place to ensure the pin book stays closed.

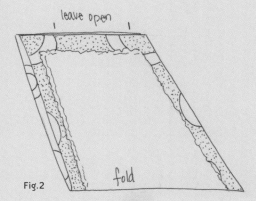
Fig. 2

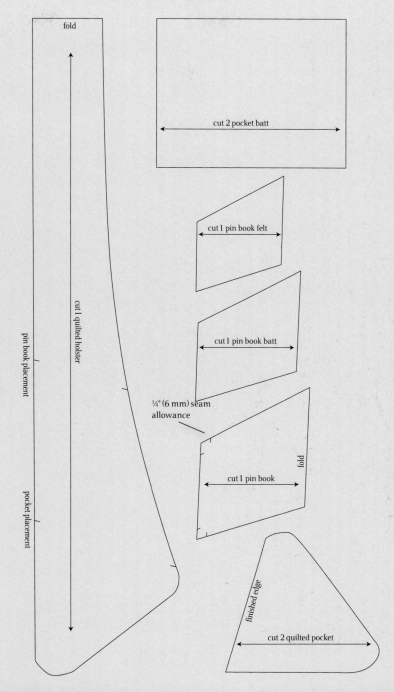

Merit Badges

Merit badges or patches are a gift that I can make for my husband, who was raised in a military family and served in the Air Force; my husband understands the value of a patch or badge. These badges are made to give value to certain events, say thank you, and remind him of my love. I sew them in the inside of his coats and to the inside flap of his daily bag. Some of these badges are intensely beaded and even have sequins. I am sure that you, too, have someone who is deserving of a merit badge or two.

To make a badge, you'll need:

- Fabrics of your own making just larger than circle template (see below)
- Batting
- Backing fabric
- Sewing machine
- Circle template (see below), enlarged to 130%
- Pins
- Scissors
- Hand-dyed embroidery floss

Grog Drinkin' Pirate Hippo

Love Bird

Hippo Drummer

Geese

Pattern for Merit Badge project using craft paper for reuse. Enlarge to 130%.

You will create your merit badge about ½" (1.3 cm) larger than your pattern piece and square. After quilting, the badge can be cut using the pattern.

1. Create image. Batch and wash.
2. Collage.
3. Sandwich the fabric, batting and backing, and quilt.
4. Place the circle template over the quiltlette and pin.
5. Cut it out.
6. Straight stitch at a ⅛" (3 mm) seam allowance.
7. Whipstitch the edge with floss to finish.

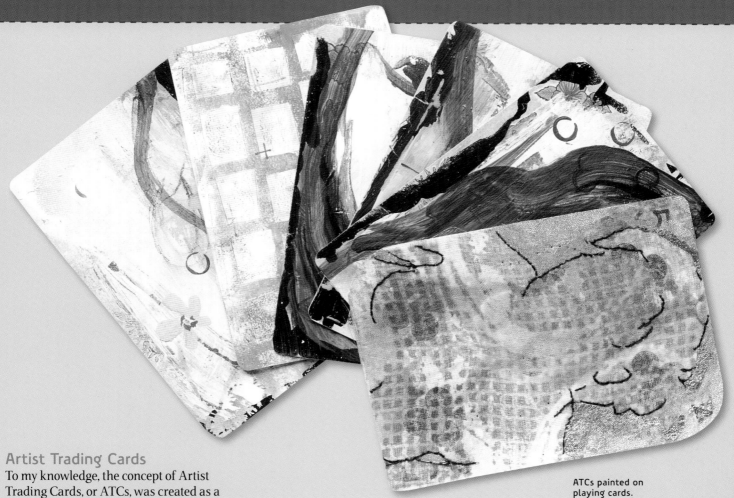

ATCs painted on playing cards.

Artist Trading Cards

To my knowledge, the concept of Artist Trading Cards, or ATCs, was created as a way to get artists out of their studios and trading, not selling, small pieces (2½" × 3½" [6.5 × 9 cm]) of art. The size of the work is easy to complete and easy to give away. These cards can be made in any media; only the size has a specific rule. For some, trading these cards in person is key; for others, trading through the Internet or by mail is just as good.

My journey into making ATCs began as a mixed-media exercise, and at that time I preferred using the back of a playing card as a base or foundation. I have never felt constrained by size; in fact, quite the opposite. I began playing with the idea of creating several cards as a single image, only to be traded separately, thus making them even more desirable.

Because the ATC is so small, I prefer the knife-edge binding. Upon finishing your last bit of machine quilting, the piece is complete and ready to trade!

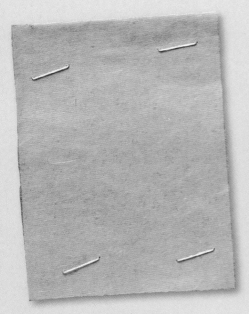

Reusable craft paper pattern for ATC.
Enlarge to 108%.

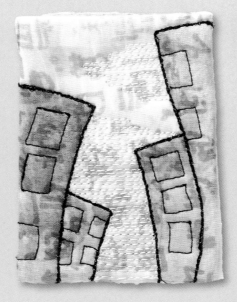

City Dwelling

Back of *City Dwelling*

To create ATCs, you'll need:

• Fabric of your own making
• Pattern (see above), enlarged to 108%
• Batting
• Fabric backing

1. Create fabric at least 2" (5 cm) larger on four sides than the pattern.
2. Batch and wash.
3. Collage.
4. Follow the directions for the knife-edge binding (see page 106).
5. Quilt.

You are ready to trade.

By Ending, You Begin Again

Allow the ideas presented in the pages of this book to cogitate and come to fruition. Creating artwork is about trust, a willingness to grow and expand, and perseverance. Consider making art a practice or custom; the expression of your creativity is a study and a lifetime pursuit. What you intend to create may or may not be what you actually make. Along the path, creative problems will surface and find resolution; new questions will arise. And again, seek resolution. Through this process, you will gain a new understanding of the tools and techniques presented here, and you will supersede them. Trust the process and embrace the learning curves.

Goose Migration (Leaving)

Goose Migration (Return)

It is my hope that you will find inspiration in these pages, but also that this book will act as a springboard, that you will find joy, solace, and pride in your own visual journals, and that you will discover new ways to interpret those ideas in cloth. I encourage you to play with both paint and dye, liberate your fear of drawing, let go, and mix color. But most important of all—get to the business of making the art that already resides within you. Immerse yourself in the processes that touch you deeply, then read and reread the sections in this book that might further your development as an artist. Make time for your creative self and allow yourself time to bloom.

There is an ebb and a flow to the creative process. Allow it to unfold. Be present and willing to embrace this aspect of being an artist. Making art and being artistic is a continuum; it doesn't stop with the last stitch. There is no opus, no final great work of art that will transcend you to a level beyond that of the common human being. There is only the *practice* of making art, getting dirty, drawing what you see, interpreting it, analyzing it, using color, and explaining new ideas.

So get to work, my friend—one day, one brushstroke, one page, and one piece of art at a time.

Gallery of Small Examples

Finding the motif and subject matter that works for you is a matter of artistic dialogue with yourself. What works for me is based on years of interaction with the world that surrounds *me*. The subject matter that satisfies and tempts me to make a piece of art may bore you. Being an artist is a journey. Finding your way and learning to express yourself is the result of that journey. Trust that the subject matter that touches you deeply will come. Make mistakes, experiment, and allow yourself to blunder, knowing that you will find your path.

Expand upon what you have learned within these pages and make these techniques your own. It is my hope that you will take these skills, learn and grow, experiment with them, and supersede my ability and approach.

And don't forget—it is perfectly acceptable to make cloth for no discernable purpose. Hopefully, you have a stash of your own fabrics that you can use to create the Pretty Purse, the Sewing Holster, the Merit Badge, or the Artist Trading Cards (see pages 110–117). The purse and sewing holster can be made separately or as a set.

The holster has pockets and a needle book and is designed to hang around your neck for quick access to all your handsewing tools. If you make the purse to match, you can carry beads and embroidery flosses wherever you go, finishing a wall hanging in style and in public, if you so choose.

Yellowstone Chair, 5" × 8½" (13 × 22.5 cm). Freezer-paper-resist chair (both layers), monoprinted, direct-dye-painted chair, chicken scratch, whipstitched binding.

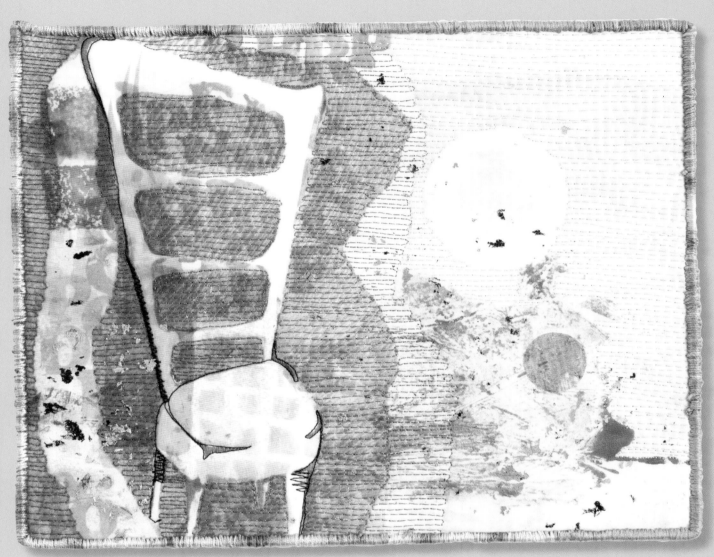

Odd Chair, 8" × 10¼" (20 × 26 cm). Organza:
Freezer-paper-resist chair, monoprinted, thick-
and-thin line. Broadcloth: Soy-wax circle,
stamped, monoprinted. Organza cut away to
expose cotton, machine quilting, whipstitched
border.

Giant Chair, Tiny Home,
9½" × 6" (24 × 15 cm).
Organza: Freezer-
paper-resist chair,
monoprinted, thick-and-
thin line. Broadcloth:
Freezer-paper-resist Os,
monoprinted, stamped.
Collage, embroidery,
machine quilting,
whipstitched binding.

Long-Legged Chair, 5¾" × 8½" (14.5 × 21.5 cm). Freezer-paper-resist chair (both layers), cotton layer printed with "O" stamp, thick-and-hin line on organza, machine quilting, whipstitched binding.

City Chair, 5" × 8" (12.5 × 20 cm). Organza: Freezer-paper-resist skyline and chair, monoprinted rust color cityscape, removed skyline and chair resist, freezer-paper-resist cityscape and arrow, monoprinted sky. Broadcloth: Freezer-paper-resist chair and arrow, monoprinted. Tracing-paper drawing skyline, organza overlay to create clouds, machine quilting, knife-edge binding.

Country Chair, 5" × 8" (12.5 × 20 cm). Organza: Freezer-paper-resist skyline and chair, monoprinted. Broadcloth: Monoprinted, stamped. Machine quilting, cushion/organza cut away, knife-edge binding.

Dancing Chair, 8" × 9½" (20 × 24 cm). Organza: Freezer-paper-resist chair, monoprinted, thick-and-thin line. Broadcloth: Soy wax, monoprinted, stamped. Machine quilting, tracing-paper drawing, beading, whipstitched binding.

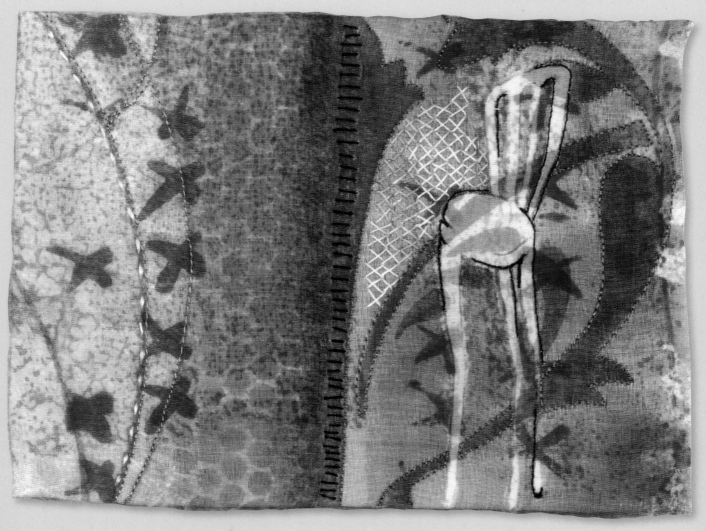

Rococo Chair, 4½" × 6" (11.5 × 15 cm). Organza: Freezer-paper-resist chair, monoprinted, printed through "honey comb ribbon." Broadcloth: Freezer-paper-stencil scroll, freezer-paper-stencil Xs, monoprinted. Embroidery, machine quilting, knife-edge binding.

Many of the chemicals we use to color and print on cloth are hazardous to our health. Knowing the limits of the media is of utmost importance to each and every one of us as artists. We need to safeguard our health while at the same time be able to create artwork for many years to come. A few precautions should be taken each time chemicals are mixed or handled.

Ethereal Shrike, 11" × 8½" (28 × 21.5 cm). Organza: Freezer-paper-resist bird and circles, monoprint. Broadcloth: Freezer-paper-resist bird and circles, monoprint. Stamp. Collage, gradation machine quilting, machine embroidery, and whipstitched binding.

Procion MX (fiber-reactive) dyes are synthetic dye powders and should be handled with respect. A dust mask and rubber gloves should be worn every time you handle these powders. Once the powders have been submerged in water and mixed thoroughly, they become stable. Once mixed, the mask can be taken off. Gloves should be worn at all times, even though dye is not absorbed through the skin.

Drips of dye will dry out and become powder once again. Dye in powder form is an irritant and should not be allowed to become airborne. Clean spills as soon as they occur to alleviate this problem entirely. Urea can cause skin and eye irritation. Use gloves and a dust mask when handling this chemical. Wash your hands thoroughly after use.

Sodium alginate is a food-grade thickener made of seaweed. You do not want to inhale this—wear a mask.

Soda ash (sodium carbonate) requires use of an MSHA/NIOSH-approved respirator with cartridges when handling this product. Wash your hands thoroughly after contact.

When handling soda-soaked and drip-dried cloth, wear a mask. Ripping or cutting this cloth will release the soda ash powder into the air. Protect your lungs.

Synthrapol should be handled with care; it can irritate the skin and eyes. It also contains alcohol, which makes it flammable.

Disposable dust masks will protect from dust and airborne irritants and are a good choice if you handle dye occasionally. Store your masks in an airtight container.

MSHA/NIOSH-approved respirator with cartridges are the best choice if you handle dye powders often. This mask fits snugly over both your mouth and your nose and will not allow dye particles to enter your lungs. This type of mask also protects your lungs from fumes. It should be stored in an airtight container because the cartridges will continue to filter the air surrounding them. The cartridges should be changed every 4 to 6 months.

Gloves should be worn at all times; dye is not absorbed through the skin, though it will stain your skin. Medical latex gloves, dishwashing gloves, or nitrile gloves (tougher than rubber) are all good choices.

Whenever introducing a new chemical into your dye studio, locate the MSDS or Material Data Safety Sheet for that product; these can be obtained directly from the retail purchase point or online. The information found on the MSDS covers everything you need to know to protect yourself in cases of inhalation, ingestion, spills, and flammability, among others. I suggest you acquire an MSDS for every applicable product in your studio. Inform yourself of the products' requirements and store these sheets in your binder for future reference.

:: Do not shake containers containing powders prior to opening them.
:: Do not eat or drink in your dye studio.
:: Do not use containers, utensils, or supplies used to dye for food preparation; it is best to keep the dye studio and the kitchen separate.
:: Wipe up spills of powders and liquids as soon as they occur.
:: Do not allow children to participate in mixing dyes and auxiliaries. Keep animals clear, too.
:: Create methodical practices when handling any of the products listed here. Close containers firmly and as quickly as possible. Store all containers in a clean and dry environment.
:: Remember, time spent in your studio should be fun, inspirational, and rewarding—and, most of all, safe. Following a few precautions to protect yourself and your supplies will ensure that your creative time is well spent.

Batching: The process of allowing dye to fully saturate printed cloth. Batching is achieved by placing soda-soaked and fiber-reactive-dye-printed cloth in a plastic bag and allowing it to set anywhere from 4 hours to several days at a time. Heat can aid the process. The optimal batch temperature is between 95° and 105°F (35° and 41°C).

Binder (three-ring binder): Use this for any paper that needs a three-hole punch. MSDS sheets, rip sheets from the pages of magazines, and design ideas that are too large to be stored in your journal get stored here. Anything and everything you might want to refer to while in your studio can go in your binder.

Burying a knot: Create a knot at the end of a piece of thread. Pass the needle through the work from the back. A quick tug will bury the knot between the layers of the quilt sandwich.

Buttonhole stitch: Buttonhole stitch is created intermittent to whipstitching when embroidering edges to finish. To create this stitch, bring the needle up from the back of the work (1), catch, and pass your needle through the loop (2) before tightening the thread to move on to your next stitch. Several of these stitches in a row will create a ridge that flows over the edge of the whipstitched border to the back of the work.

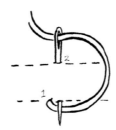

Chocolate: A needed divergence and supplement to making great art.

Clean finish: This finish completely hides a raw edge. Turn half your seam allowance under once, then one additional time. Sew the turned edge down.

Drip-dried: Soda-soaked fabric that has been drip-dried.

Dye concentrate: A highly concentrated liquid mixture of Procion MX dye, water, and urea. See recipe on page 16.

Ghost print: Most often occurs when monoprinting; after the first print is transferred to your intended cloth, dye may be left on the plate. Printing from this will give a lighter, less exact, ghost print.

Gimp: A heavy cord or thread, traditionally having a metal core. Gimp is used to strengthen whipstitched bindings. Yarn and heavy-duty string make good substitutes.

Gold foil: A Mylar sheet with a metallic surface coating. This metallic coating is released from the Mylar sheet and bonded to cloth with glue.

Gold leaf: Imitation gold leaf is available much more readily than the real stuff. Gold leaf is sold in book format. Individual sheets are tucked into the diaphanous pages of a pad of paper. Gold leaf will blow away with the slightest movement. Keep the book closed until use.

Journal: Contains watercolor-type paper on which to make doodles and collage. This is a place to retreat artistically in the medium of your choice.

Monoprint: A form of printing that cannot be easily reproduced; usually just a single print can be obtained. For our purposes, dye is applied to a plate (either Plexiglas or plastic sheeting); dye can be removed, textured, or added to this plate until you achieve a successful result. Cloth is then applied to the plate, brayered, and removed. At that point, the dye has been transferred from the plate to the cloth. If an additional print can be obtained, it is because the cloth did not absorb the entire application of dye from the plate. The resulting second print is called a ghost print.

Partial sandwich: This is useful when the organza layer will act to secure design elements. The organza layer is held aside and the quilt sandwich is created in order to give substance to stitch or collage applications.

PFD (prepared for dye): PFD cloth has been scoured, bleached, and de-sized but does not have optical brighteners or softeners, which can interfere with a dye's ability to penetrate the fiber.

Plexiglass or plastic sheeting: Also called a plate; these two items can be used as a surface on which to create monoprints.

Print board: A padded surface suitable for printing techniques such as stamping, screen printing, and direct-dye painting. Print paste: A mixture of sodium alginate, urea, and water softener.

Procion MX dyes: A cold reactive type of dye. For optimal results, dye baths and batching temperatures should reach 95° to 105°F (35° to 41°C). The name Procion MX is a proprietary name. The more appropriate name for this dye now is Procion MX–type dye and is synonymously called fiber-reactive dye.

Professional textile detergent: Dharma Trading's alternative to Synthrapol is nontoxic and alcohol free.

Pro Print Paste F: PRO Chemical's proprietary mixture of sodium alginate, urea, and water softener. This is specifically formulated for use on silk. F is formulated to have a low viscosity.

Pro Print Paste SH: PRO Chemical's proprietary mixture of sodium alginate, urea, and water softener. This is specifically formulated for use on cotton, although it also works on silks. SH is formulated to have a high viscosity.

Resist: A resist can be any object or media that prevents dye from entering into and reacting with cloth.

Running stitch: The running stitch is a basic sewing stitch created by passing the needle in and out of the quilt top at even intervals. Beads can be attached in this manner as long as you tie off often.

Satin stitch: A narrow row of stitches used to completely conceal an area of cloth.

Soda ash (sodium carbonate): Used as an alkali fixative with reactive dyes.

Soda soak: To soak cloth in a soda ash solution. See recipe on page 19.

Sodium alginate: A food-grade thickener made of seaweed.

Sodium alginate HV (high viscosity): A food-grade thickener made of seaweed. This is Dharma Trading's designation for sodium alginate geared toward use on cotton fabrics.

Sodium alginate LV (low viscosity): A food-grade thickener made of seaweed. This is Dharma Trading's designation for sodium alginate geared toward use on silk fabrics.

Soy wax: A plant-based wax with a low melt temperature of 180°F (82°C). It can be washed with no adverse affects in your home washing machine and is used as a resist.

Stamp: A cut, carved, or molded surface where dye or paint is applied and transferred to cloth or paper. Some stamp surfaces need to be mounted to stabilize them for repeated use.

Synthrapol: A type of detergent formulated to isolate and remove dye particles in the wash cycle.

Thickener: Also known as sodium alginate, a food-grade thickener made of seaweed.

Urea (synthetic): Used as a humectant, allowing the cloth to stay wet and absorbent for long periods of time. This allows the dye a more prolonged period to react with the fiber. Because of these attributes, we use urea water as white in color mixing with Procion MX (fiber-reactive) dyes. Urea is sold in tiny pellets or crystals.

Urea water: Used as white in color mixing with Procion MX (fiber-reactive) dyes. See recipe on page 18.

Washing: Removing thickener, dyes, and chemicals from your printed cloth by first soaking in cold water until the water runs clear, then washing in a washing machine using hot water. Synthrapol or professional textile detergent should be used in the hot wash cycle.

Whipstitch: A type of edge finish. Whipstitches bind an edge together, concealing the raw edges. The stitches should be closely spaced. Knot your embroidery floss, threading it from the front of the work. Whip the needle around to the back of the work; bring the needle up alongside your previous stitch (Figure 1), burying the tail as you continue on (Figure 2).

Fig. 1

Fig. 2

Cartwright Sequins and Beads
11108 North Hwy. 348
Mountainburg, AR 74926
ccartwright.com
A great place for sequins—flat, square, tiny, and large.

American Frame Corporation
400 Tomahawk Drive
Maumee, OH 43537
americanframe.com
(888) 628-3833
Build frames, shadow boxes, and more!

Creative Illuminations
aka Gelluminations Inc.
11959 240th Avenue
Spirit Lake, IA 51360
creativeilluminations.com
(866) 776-4355
Pillar-type soy wax in bulk.

Dharma Trading
PO Box 150916
San Rafael, CA 94915
dharmatrading.com
(800) 542-5227
Auxiliaries, dyes, cloth, and tools with a down-to-earth, informative catalog.

PRO Chemical & Dye
PO Box 14
Somerset, MA 02726
prochemical.com
(800) 228-9393
Auxiliaries, dyes, and tools with a practical, supportive approach and classes to boot.

Robison-Anton
PO Box 507
22 American Street
Mount Holly, NC 28120
robison-anton.com
(800) 847-3235
Super strength rayon thread, shiny, yummy candy!

Testfabrics
PO Box 26
West Pittiston, PA 18643
testfabrics.com
(570) 603-0432
Cottons, silks, rayons, and more in bulk.

Thai Silks
252 State Street
Los Altos, CA 94022
thaisilks.com
(800) 722-7455
The silk gauze here is beautilous!

Treenway Silks
501 Musgrave Road
Salt Spring Island, BC
Canada V8K 1V5
treenwaysilks.com
(888) 383-7455
Undyed silk flosses, ribbons, and fiber.

Zipper Stop
27 Allen Street
New York, NY 10002
zipperstop.com
(888) 947-7872
Zipper bling, rhinestones, and Riri zippers.

I would also like to thank my mentors and teachers who have affected and directed my creative path. I suggest you check these artists and teachers out for the sake of informing yourself.

Jane Dunnewold
artclothstudios.com

Natasha Kempers-Cullen
natashakempers-cullen.com

Carol Soderlund
carolsoderlund.com

David Walker
davidwalker.us

Ann Johnston
annjohnston.net

Baptiste Ibar
baptisteibar.com

Danny Gregory
dannygregory.com

John Copeland (especially his journals)
johncopeland.com

Sabrina Ward Harrison
sabrinawardharrison.com/ee

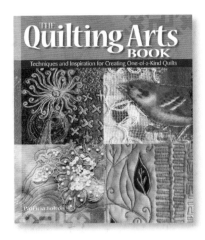
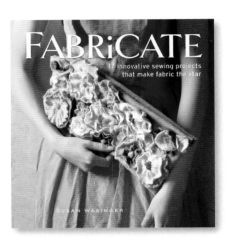
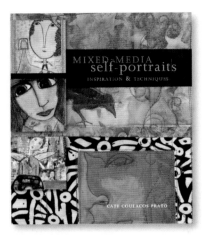